PRAISE for MARGOT MURPHY and *VITALIZE YOUR WORKFORCE*

"I have worked with Margot Murphy for over twenty-five years as a colleague, client, and consultant. On various engagements I have marveled at her ingenuity, analytical problem solving, and resourcefulness. I have witnessed her successfully engage with all levels of management from Fortune 100 clients to Silicon Valley entrepreneurs. Her approach is always straightforward, engaging, and professional."

– Joe Griffin, Managing Partner of GCS-Team, LLC

"As an author myself of more than fifty books on strategy, I must emphasize how much I learned from reading *Vitalize Your Workforce*. With many of my own books, once you put them down, you just can't pick them up! With Margot Murphy's book, however, the very opposite is true. Not only is she an excellent and engaging writer, but she writes in short, to-the-point chapters that contain actionable propositions, so readers can experience the whole process in gentle, easy-to-assimilate stages. The world will be a much better place as a result of her work."

– Professor Malcolm McDonald MA (Oxon), MSc, PhD, Dlitt, DSc, Emeritus Professor, Cranfield University School of Management

"Today, more than ever, employees are stagnant in their jobs and performing the minimum tasks each day because they don't share in their company's vision, hence don't feel a future for themselves. In *Vitalize Your Workforce*, Margot Murphy provides an integrated fabric of solutions for executive and supervisor leadership to transform employee stagnation into sustainable application of employees' true potential. This book offers insight for all levels of management."

– Scott K. Erickson, S K Erickson Consulting LLC

"In *Vitalize Your Workforce,* Margot Murphy gets to the truths that lie behind employee stagnation and how you can transform it into a vitalized workforce. She offers a realistic picture of corporate America today and a visionary, yet practical view of how organizations will look in 2020 and beyond."

— Tyler R. Tichelaar, PhD and award-winning author of
Narrow Lives and *The Best Place*

"Your organization is destined to improve, moving from employee stagnation to a vitalized workforce where everyone is productive and knows their value of working for you. This is your moment of destiny when you decide to read this book and put its concepts to work."

— Patrick Snow, publishing coach and
international best-selling author of *The Affluent Entrepreneur*

VITALIZE
Your **workforce**

Conquering the Crisis of Employee Stagnation

MARGOT M MURPHY
with Dr James A Robertson

AVIVA
PUBLISHING
New York

Vitalize Your Workforce
Conquering the Crisis of Employee Stagnation

© 2019 MARGOT M. MURPHY

Thank you for purchasing an authorized copy of this book and for complying with copyright laws.

All rights reserved. No portions of this book may be reproduced, stored in a retrieval system, or transmitted in any form or by any means—electronic, mechanical, photocopy, recording, scanning, or other—except for brief quotations in critical reviews or articles, without the prior written permission of the publisher.

Liability Disclaimer: Human progress and accomplishment take hard work. As stipulated by law, we cannot and do not make any guarantees about your ability to get results or earn money with our ideas, information, tools, or strategies. The publisher and author specifically disclaim any implied warranties of merchantability or fitness for a particular purpose and make no guarantees whatsoever that you will achieve a particular result. Any case studies presented herein do not necessarily represent what you will achieve since success depends on a variety of factors. All the case studies and results presented herein are true and accurate, but we have not audited the results. The advice and strategies contained in this book may not even be suitable for your situation, and you should consult your own advisors as appropriate. The publisher and author shall not be held liable for any loss of profit or any other commercial damages, including but not limited to special, incidental, consequential, or other damages. The fact that an organization or website is referred to in this work as a citation and/or potential source of information does not mean that the publisher or author endorse the information the organization or website may provide or the recommendations they may make. Further, readers should be aware that internet websites listed in this work may have changed or disappeared after this work was written.

Editor: Superior Book Productions
Cover design: Lisa Vento Hainline, www.lisahainline.com
Production assistance from TLC Book Design, TLCBookDesign.com

Published in New York, New York, by Aviva Publishing.

ISBN: 978-1-947937-59-8

Library of Congress Control Number: 2018907927

ACKNOWLEDGMENTS

SINCERE THANKS AND APPRECIATION TO DR. JAMES A. Robertson, PhD, international consultant in IT, ERP, and strategic change for helping design and develop new solutions for the pervasive problem of employee stagnation. Dr. Robertson's ability to think outside the box while applying engineering disciplines to critical leadership and human motivation issues has provided an important foundation for assessing, addressing, and resolving employee stagnation on a fundamental level.

Dr. Robertson's dedicated collaboration to help write this book, refine the Vitality Consulting platform, design the Vitalize Corporate Vitality Assessment software, and oversee its development is invaluable. Our original intention to create and provide a sustainable new paradigm for Vitality Leadership with new methods to unleash the captive, unrealized potential of employees and create a new competitive edge for 2020 is now here.

I thank Dan Vogel for his partnership and important contribution to proving the practical application of this work; Nicolaas Hugo for his dedicated strategic software development and IT architecture expertise; Teresa Larsen, PhD for her critical attention to ensuring high quality data analysis and reporting for our Corporate Vitality Assessment process; Rahul Chopra for his tireless research and analysis support; Mark Porteous for his consistent, insightful high value as my personal coach, helping me stay on track with my goals for the book and development of the Vitalize business; Lana McCara for her editorial coaching and professional encouragement in the first year of this important endeavor; and Pamela Day for her friendship and editorial assistance with this manuscript.

CONTENTS

Preface .... *xiii*
Foreword .... *xv*
Introduction *1*

SECTION 1	THE CRISIS OF EMPLOYEE STAGNATION 9
Chapter 1:	The Crisis of Employee Stagnation… Is Loud and Clear 11
Chapter 2:	Stagnant or Vitalized? 19
Chapter 3:	Real Change Requires Measurement 27
Case Study:	*Measurement Resolves Discordant Communication Among C-Levels* *28*

SECTION 2	VITALIZE ISSUE RESOLUTION AND PROBLEM SOLVING 35
Chapter 4:	Problem Solving IS a Problem 37
Case Study:	**John: A True Problem Solver** 38
Chapter 5:	People Problems May Be Process Problems— Look Deeper! 47
Case Study:	*Medical Office* *47*
Chapter 6:	Vitalizing Vertical and Horizontal Communication 55
Case Study:	*Supply Chain Problem* *55*
Chapter 7:	Confronting Negativity Head-On— Mission Critical! 61
Chapter 8:	Embedding Critical Issue Resolution and Problem Solving 69

SECTION 3	**SHARED LEARNING CREATES VITALITY**	**79**
Chapter 9:	Cross-Training Is Shared Learning	81
Chapter 10:	Dynamic Delegation	87
Chapter 11:	Establishing Universal Mentoring	99
SECTION 4	**WHAT'S IN IT FOR ME?**	**111**
Chapter 12:	Activating Appreciation	113
Chapter 13:	Recognition and Celebration	123
Chapter 14:	Creating Continual Opportunity	133
SECTION 5	**THE ENERGIZING POWER OF PROGRESSIVE INCENTIVES**	**139**
Chapter 15:	Progressive Incentives Create Reach	141
Case Study:	Frank	148
Chapter 16:	A Living Fabric of Incentives	153
Chapter 17:	Creating and Managing Integrated Incentives	161
Chapter 18:	Meaningful Rewards Create Loyalty	173
SECTION 6	**TAKE CHARGE**	**181**
Chapter 19:	Introducing a Chief Vitality Officer C-Level Position	183
Chapter 20:	Discovering the Strategic Essence of Your Organization	193
Case Study:	**Freight Clearing Agent**	**196**
Chapter 21:	Vitalizing Your Vision	201
Chapter 22:	Magnifying Your Mission	209

Case Study:	Publix... 211
Chapter 23:	Kick-Starting Your Culture 219
Case Study:	**Campbell's Soup**............................... **223**
Case Study:	Lawrence...................................... 225
Chapter 24:	Enlivening Your Policies......................... 235
Chapter 25:	Finding and Activating Your Real People-Leaders 243

SECTION 7 VITALIZE YOUR FOCUS 251

Chapter 26:	Measuring Vitality Is an Imperative 253
Chapter 27:	Future Perfect in a Vitalized Organization 263
Chapter 28:	The Critical Factors in Vitalizing Your Workforce....................... 279

A Final Note—Leading for Vitality Guarantees Success............ 289

New Vocabulary..*293*
Research References...*305*
Index...*309*

Vitality

The inherent meaning of *vitality* is "vital life force."
Vitality is the creative energy of life.
Does your company have it?

PREFACE

AS A GLOBAL STRATEGY EXPERT, MY ROLE IS TO SHOW ORGAnizations how to develop strategies that create value for all stakeholders, not just for shareholders. Over the years, however, I have been disappointed that many of them are poorly implemented.

Recently, my colleagues and I conducted a survey of senior executives in seventy organizations to find out why. Over 40 percent of respondents reported losing more than 10 percent of their profits and 20 percent were losing 15 percent or more of their profits. The two overwhelming reasons given were:

"Our organisation itself (including its structure, culture, metrics processes, and rewards mechanisms)"

"Our Human Resources (at all levels, their commitment, ability, and resourcing levels)"

The sad fact is that this situation is undoubtedly a multibillion-dollar problem. If we apply the above percentages to the top fifty American corporations, we estimate the total lost profits from strategy implementation failure to be well over $50 billion. Add to that the lost profits from the thousands of companies further down the American chain and you can see the size of the potential global goldmine available to us.

Whilst I have devoted some of my professional life to trying to understand why perfectly sound, agreed strategies often fail to get implemented, it wasn't until recently when I had the privilege of discovering the lifelong work of Margot Murphy that the veil was lifted for me. It is one thing to understand *which* problems get in the way. It is entirely another matter to understand *what* needs to be done to solve them. This is precisely what Margot Murphy has done in this truly brilliant book.

As an author myself of more than fifty books on strategy, I must emphasize how much I learned from reading *Vitalize Your Workforce*. With many of my own books, once you put them down, you just can't pick them up! With Margot Murphy's book, however, the very opposite is true. Not only is she an excellent and engaging writer, but she has written it in short, to-the-point chapters that contain actionable propositions, so readers can experience the whole process in gentle, easy-to-assimilate stages.

I am so thrilled to know Margot Murphy after all these years, and I wish I had met her years ago. The world will be a much better place as a result of her work.

Professor Malcolm McDonald MA (Oxon) MSc PhD DLitt DSc
Emeritus Professor,
Cranfield University School of Management

Correspondence to: 72 Churchway, Haddenham, Bucks HP17 8HA
Telephone: +44 (0) 1844 291458
Email: m.mcdonald@cranfield.ac.uk

FOREWORD

FOLLOWING A LONG CAREER WITH FORTUNE 500 COMPANIES in eleven industries, including four blue-chip companies, it was time to apply my talents to benefit others in a new way.

Throughout my career, I witnessed the pervasiveness of employee lack of engagement, firsthand. Frustrated by this languishing potential and wanting greater understanding, I recently traveled the country for a year offering 130 seminars on eight different subjects to over 2,400 participants in fifteen states. These participants included employees from hundreds of companies at every level, top to bottom, ranging from presidents, CEOs, directors, middle-management, supervisors, production workers, cashiers, and more.

Underlying the conversations with all the participants was a consistent message. They weren't disengaged; they were stagnant. Regardless of how I reformulated my questions, hoping to receive different answers, I kept getting exactly the same responses: "I am busy, but don't feel connected to the company…"; "There is no future for me here, I just stay for the benefits..."; "Managers don't solve problems, so why should I care?" In light of this discovery, I realized there was an immense need for a real achievable solution.

These were good employees in real pain within their work situations. Each felt he or she had no way up, except to leave. Most felt they were merely an unappreciated headcount.

I started asking deeper questions, probing for insight into their situations. The results were striking. What emerged was a consistent pattern that pointed to a single root cause: Companies are unintentionally strangling the very human potential they pay good wages and salaries to hire and retain. Employees are dumbed down and numbed out in their hearts, desperately wanting to express more of themselves and contribute more meaningfully to the organization's greater good. Millions of people in this country have given up and are staying in positions where they are unhappy, for lack of a better choice or for the benefits they can't afford to lose. Organizational cultures have settled so deeply that mediocrity has taken over.

There is an epic struggle nationwide for employees to release themselves from stagnation, and for organizations to recognize and leverage their employees' personal potential. *Vitalize Your Workforce* will enable you to move past the present epidemic of stagnation and create a new paradigm for business effectiveness in a changing world with accelerating demands. This paradigm will be founded on a high-value partnership between the organization and its people.

Vitalize Your Workforce brings together a diversity of disciplines that collectively address every facet of the employee stagnation problem. Starting with this book, we introduce the scope of the problem together with a comprehensive selection of tools and techniques that address strategic leadership and operational issues to deliver a vitalized and highly competitive, transformed organization.

We introduce the role of a Chief Vitality Officer dedicated to defining and implementing the Vitalize Your Workforce principles and practices throughout your organization. We offer a proprietary Corporate Vitality Assessment software that helps you understand where and how deep the problem is in your organization and enables you to prioritize next steps. We offer new shared learning programs that integrate and instill the fundamentals of issue resolution, problem solving, and other collaborative skills to continually build employee perspectives, confidence, and involvement.

This all takes place within the context of a tailored strategic view of your organization's requirements. We work with you and your leadership team to ensure the resolution of stagnation with sustainable, transformative programs that are easy to understand, broadly applicable, and cost effective.

The Vitality Assessment Software measures the level of employee stagnation and vitality within the organization at every level using proprietary scientific metrics. This makes it possible for every company to understand the severity of the problem and where it resides. Vitality measurements will enable focused application of the Vitalize methods to activate the human potential within each worker. Productivity and creativity can be unleashed on a scale that, untapped up to now, has been seen in only a handful of companies.

In a Vitalized Workforce, energized employees are excited to come to work and apply their personal motivation to the organization's Vision and Mission. This means they are confident and expanding their ability to care for themselves and their families and to contribute to the job at hand. As a result, the competitiveness, flexibility, sustainability, and profitability of the organization soars.

I invite you to join me on this exciting journey as we discuss in detail exactly how to "Vitalize Your Workforce" and unleash the full potential of your people.

Margot M. Murphy
Somerville, New Jersey

"If your actions inspire others to dream more, learn more, do more, and become more, you are a leader."

– John Quincy Adams

INTRODUCTION

THE TERM "EMPLOYEE ENGAGEMENT" IS DEAD. THE CONCEPT is old, worn out, and worst of all, unresolved—and the situation is getting worse.

The converging dynamics of encroaching world chaos, accelerating technologies, differing generational values and disciplines, plus decades of programmed and enforced employee stagnation are creating an almost insurmountable morass of complexity challenging vision, leadership, and even survival. According to an April 2017 Mercer Study on Global Talent Trends,[1] 93 percent of organizations worldwide report they are planning to redesign their structure in the next two years, and only 4 percent of business executives say they are change-ready.

Are you ready or looking the other way? What are you doing right now to create a new vital competitive edge?

> "The moment we believe that success is determined by an ingrained level of ability as opposed to resilience and hard work, we will be brittle in the face of adversity."[2]
>
> – JOSHUA WAITZKIN

Corporate Vitality is mandatory to manage and succeed through this increasing quagmire of influence. It requires thinking about employee potential a different way. It requires a different way of communicating and interacting within your organization, rethinking training, redesigning reward…*everything*. We need to step back and rethink everything we took for granted about our organizations, and then rethink it again.

Start with some well-known statistics from Gallup and add some If/Then scenarios:

- **If:** 52 percent (approximately 156 million) of Americans work for companies with 500 or more employees,[3]

    Then: how big is our real responsibility to America?

- **If:** 85 percent or more (approximately 136 million) of these employees feel apathetic or antagonistic toward their employer,[4]

    Then: where is your organization's strength?

- **If:** Two-thirds of working Americans have been disengaged in some form or fashion for the past fifteen years,

    Then: we have five generations or more of people passing on "can't do, won't do, and just staying for the benefits" thinking.

- **If:** You know this eroding malaise is actually decades longer and deeper than that,

    Then: what do you have to work with?

- **If:** There is a growing "great divide" between companies with executives accelerating redesign of their organizations for competitive vitality and confidence, and those who are not,

    Then: where are you? Where do you want to be? Where do you need to be?

These are serious questions. Employee stagnation is a mold. It is silent, invasive, and pervasive. It is present all the time and increasingly visible as seven-figure garage startups appear out of nowhere, fracturing market share overnight. How fast can your company recover from terrorist activity that threatens your location? How fast can you apply new technologies that gain the attention of the best and the brightest? What happens when you look around to see who is ready, and very few of your employees are? How does that feel?

So, what do I mean by "Vitality"?

I am referring to a change in the attitude and state of mind of your workforce—from the most junior to the most senior levels—a state of mind that welcomes accountability, exercises initiative, and seeks to grow the employee and the organization simply because it can. Research shows that motivated and committed employees can increase the profitability of their organization by a factor of 2.5 times.[5]

> *"It is proven via many studies from across the world that when you have a great workplace, the profit of your business or team should increase by up to 2.5 times. Literally... Sales are up to 20 percent higher for an engaged team member, customer service provided is "up the scale," and shareholders are well, very happy!"*[6]
>
> — ZAC DE SILVA

Surviving in this economic climate requires a new model—a model designed to create and sustain vitality. A model where we stay light on our feet, moving easily to meet and rise above each challenge, because we know we can.

Sound dramatic? The reality is that it may sound dramatic, but it is real. We are all feeling the pressure of unrelenting and accelerating change. We need to stand up, have a new voice, and work together to create a new paradigm of sustainable vitality.

Having held positions of significant responsibility in several global corporations, I understand that your time and attention are at an increasing premium. I am fully aware that working at a relative distance from the mass of general employees is a typical reality. I know that training and training budgets are disintegrating, and there is a temptation just to hire new talent. But…

> **What if:** 65 percent of your workforce is planning to leave your organization within the next two years if their work is not recognized?[7]

> **What if:** 50 percent of your workforce is union, with pension-eligible retirement dates based on years of service, and they don't care enough to pass on what they know?

We all know that nothing can stop the acceleration of technologies and world chaos. What can you do now to think and act differently? You can start by adopting a leadership goal to let go of business-as-usual thinking and build a Vitalized organization.

In this book, you will learn:

- The true causes of employee stagnation, how pervasive it is, and the danger of ignoring it.
- The clear difference between Stagnant and Vitalized organizations.
- The power of high-quality measurement of Corporate Vitality throughout the organization to enable clear new strategic goals for workforce transformation.
- How managed Shared Learning creates Vitality and accelerates creative thinking and problem solving.
- The power of establishing consistent, progressive, integrated incentives.
- How to implement low-risk, low-cost employee-related programs to eliminate the sludge of stagnation.
- The extraordinary value of establishing a Corporate Vitality Officer function into your organizational structure, reporting to the Chief Executive Officer.
- Leadership initiatives to Vitalize your vision, mission, culture, and policy documents.
- The ideal future state for your employees.
- Critical factors in Vitalizing Your Workforce.

This is just the beginning. When you apply the wisdom, systems, and strategies in this book, you will start building a foundation for new thought across your organization. You will accelerate your ability to respond to challenges and new opportunities with alacrity.

You will experience:

- Significant reduction of common stagnation indicators such as turnover, absenteeism, negativity, sabotage, and healthcare costs.
- An awakening of employees to the understanding that they can now stretch to experience their own potential and help create their own future while working for you.
- Confidence in your ability to effectively discern areas of stagnation and efficiently measure Vitalization anywhere, anytime, with quality, professional measuring tools.

- Employees sharing responsibility for the development of their mutual talents and readiness for new opportunities.
- The power of establishing a new, permanent Vitality Leadership function within your executive team.
- A transformation of your corporate image from business-as-usual to a progressive thinking, learning organization that exemplifies Vitality and the new, competitive edge it brings.

I don't have all the answers. However, my twenty-six years of proven hands-on business development experience enables me to see the employee stagnation problem from a different perspective. Add to that my years on competitive sports teams and as a seminar trainer covering the United States, talking with over 2,400 employees from over 200 industries and I believe I have something significant to impart to assist you in turning this serious employee stagnation situation around.

We need to start asking different questions. We need to provide new, highly practical solutions now in order to release your employees' potential and create new leadership practices that build sustainable Vitality.

Many of you are apprehensive about any program that claims to be capable of a "company-wide" application. I know that thinking about introducing any "universal programs" may raise a red flag. I know you are skeptical of their value and that you have doubts about any claims of low cost. You have likely spoken with many consultants or coaches about employee lack of engagement and their programs haven't worked. You may even believe that nothing can touch employees or make a difference. I get that. But it doesn't have to be that way.

I want to be your coach and accountability partner to help view the situation in a different way. I want to help you Vitalize your connection with your employees. I want to raise your confidence and the confidence of your employees for their own future—by working for you.

I am passionate about your success. Are you ready to begin? Are you open to new methods of thinking about your organization and your employees, in particular? Are you ready to define and achieve the new goals required to meet the ever-accelerating challenges of 2020 and beyond? If so, great! Let's get started!

PLEASE NOTE:

Some of the concepts offered here may be completely new ideas, and some may have a common name with completely new definitions. To support future dialogue and activation of the concepts, I have added notes pages after each chapter for your convenience.

You may also note that I sometimes refer to the first person "I" and sometimes I refer to "we." I have chosen to refer to "we" in areas of distinct collaboration between myself and Dr. James Robertson previously mentioned in Acknowledgments.

The references to Vitality Leadership Certification and Vitality Leadership Award Certification, recognizing organizations that have reached a qualified level of Vitality Leadership throughout their organization, are mentioned to let you know there is more coming!

"The choice facing the American people is not between growth and stagnation, but between short-term growth and long-term disaster."

— STEWART UDALL

SECTION 1
THE CRISIS OF EMPLOYEE STAGNATION

"Change is fearsome, but stagnation is lethal."
— DEBASISH MRIDHA, M.D.

CHAPTER 1

THE CRISIS OF EMPLOYEE STAGNATION… IS LOUD AND CLEAR

MANY STATISTICS SHOW THAT APPROXIMATELY 85 PERCENT of employees are disengaged.[8] This is a well-known statistic, with many years of conversation surrounding it. But the truth is the term "employee engagement" is dead.

Over the past five years, we've seen an average annual turnover of 19 percent,[9] with increasing absenteeism and skyrocketing "What's in it for me?" attitudes. In 2015, cities such as Baltimore, Maryland, experienced devastating riots resulting largely from high levels of individual stagnation. In Baltimore's Sandtown-Winchester neighborhood, more than half of the people between the ages of 16 and 64 are out of work and the unemployment rate is double that for the city at one in five,[10] a serious breakdown of family structures, and no programs designed to productively engage their neglected human potential. These situations across the country have a direct impact on the vitality and resilience of our cities and our economy.

Stagnating water, stagnating thoughts, stagnating opportunities, or stagnating people—the longer the stagnation continues, the deeper the scourge. Stagnating people first become resigned, then apathetic, then resentful, then ultimately, they rebel. It is no different at work.

"Keep asking the question: What is the cause?"

We clearly see the problem and its myriad effects, but we need to keep asking the question, "What is the cause?"

A Closer Look

Many causes of personal stagnation are so commonplace that they are easily overlooked. Some of the stagnation-generating situations that erode employee potential every day are:

- overloading employees, then taking their time and effort for granted
- placing reluctant employees in "temporary" positions, then forgetting them
- considering employees in "low-value" jobs as low-value people
- leaving employees' natural talents and interests unrecognized and untapped
- assigning issue-resolution and problem-solving authority to a select few
- not caring whether individuals don't understand how they fit into the bigger picture
- honoring formal education over natural talent
- the tendency to regard managers as "people-controllers" rather than "people-leaders"
- minimizing recognition and celebration as expensive, optional budget items
- a company culture that conveys the message, "Don't complain; just be glad you have a job."

When you hear, "This can't be all there is," "There must be something else I can do," "I'm bored," or "I just stay here for the benefits," you have unaddressed, viral stagnation. Stagnant employees invest the minimum amount of time and energy into their jobs. They stay mainly for the benefits, then go home. Is this what you want?

"Most stagnant employees do as little as possible."

When you ask stagnant employees to do more, what happens? They do as little as possible. When asked for their input, they remain silent. Does that mean they are dumb? No. They are stagnant. What is to blame for this painful stagnation? Antiquated management habits.

The Start of Reductionism (Reductionist Thinking)

In the late 1800s, Frederick Winslow Taylor experimented with ways to achieve greater production with less effort and expense. In his book *The Principles of Scientific Management,* Taylor espoused reduction of individual thought (reductionist thinking), replacing it with robotic-style conformity to increase production while decreasing errors and reducing payroll. This made statistical analysis the guiding principle of performance. Employee directives came from a few at the top. "All others" had to meet their goals on time, the same way, and in silence—or lose their jobs. Competitive success depended on adopting these principles in as many functions as possible.

For over a century, US manufacturing experienced great success by focusing on statistically-led production efficiency. We will always need efficiency, and we will always be grateful for our proven ability to manage efficiency. We won World War II because of this approach. Efficiency was the key driver that made the United States the global leader in manufacturing from the 1930s to the 1990s. It gave us the lead in developing advanced communication, food production, and space travel. Today, statistically driven efficiency is so common globally that it is no longer a competitive differentiator.

> *"Unless we fully grasp the need to lead our employees with a focus on Vitality as our new core strength, we will be left behind."*

The statistically driven efficiency model claimed that the smartest people were naturally at the top of the organization, and the rest were merely a necessary workforce. This mindset became a habit of thought reinforced over many generations. Opportunities and reward were applied to the top echelon while the rest marched in place.

The 2000s saw a driving emphasis on corporate growth and Enterprise Resource Planning (ERP) with rapidly developing mergers and acquisitions and expanding business information systems.

In the decade beginning in 2010, computer capacity became effectively unlimited, unlocking technology's full potential. Smart phones, tablets, and burgeoning applications signaled that previous business software was becoming inadequate to meet the needs of an environment that was changing at a breakneck pace. The guiding initiative became the drive to tap the technology's full potential.

The coming decade of the 2020s will be about unlocking the constraint of people and applying their potential effectively. We now face an era when a huge number of mundane jobs will be replaced by computer technology and robots or will be totally redefined. Highly computer-and social-media-savvy Gen X, Y, and Z are rejecting conventional work models, management constraints, and measurements that have been traditionally applied.

Today's employees become (directly or indirectly) resentful of reductionist thinking. With the advent of the internet, the leadership value of this approach has disintegrated. Efficiency is always necessary, but unwanted employee turnover, resistance to reductionist practices, and workforce stagnation tell a different story.

In today's tech environment, the nanosecond need for new idea generation and problem solving requires almost instantaneous collaboration in every area of the organization. Add to that the need for quick recovery from catastrophic events and the need for committed employees and Vitality becomes an imperative rather than an option.

*"We need to take action to change our own story
or change will be made for us. It is as simple as that."*

The challenge for the 2020s will be to expand and channel these newly liberated human capabilities. *Vitalize Your Workforce* is geared toward addressing this goal and enabling corporations to harness the full potential of all generations within their workforce.

CHAPTER 1
SUMMARY

THE CRISIS OF STAGNATION IS VERY REAL. WE NEED TO TAKE action and change how we think about our employees and the importance of their potential, or unwanted change in our businesses will be made for us.

The causes of employee stagnation have been around for so long they are easily overlooked. When you hear, "This can't be all there is," "There must be something else I can do," "I'm bored," or "I just stay here for the benefits," you have unaddressed, viral stagnation.

In ten short years, we have moved rapidly through the development and growth of new technologies to the ubiquitous application of those technologies, often rendering traditional business planning obsolete. We are now facing the coming decade of the 2020s, in which the focus will turn to unlocking the constraint of people and applying their potential effectively. Are you ready?

Vitalize Your Workforce is geared to address this situation directly, enabling corporations to harness the full potential of their workforce. Stagnation won't be solved overnight, but we need to take action to change our own story, or the change will be made for us by our competition. It is as simple as that.

NOTES

Actions: _____

_____

_____

_____

_____

Call Whom: _____

_____

_____

_____

By When: _____

_____

_____

_____

_____

"Don't fear criticism; fear stagnation."
— DEBASISH MRIDHA, M.D.

CHAPTER 2

STAGNANT OR VITALIZED?

THE TERMS "AGILE" AND "ENGAGED" ARE VALID IN THE CONTEXT of organizations and the people within those organizations. However, they are overused and are only a part of the essential goal we are talking about. I prefer to talk about Vitality and Vitalized employees, which is the subject of this book.

The opposite of Vitalized is stagnant—numbed out, dumbed down, demotivated, disinterested, job-seeking people who come to work because they have to earn a living and who watch the clock from the moment they arrive, earnestly desiring to be free of their captivity. Research shows that approximately 85 percent of employees in the United States are stagnant, and worse, have been for a long time. We need to look at the issue in a different way to generate a different answer and create highly responsive Vital organizations.

Vitality is not an adjective or an adverb. Vitality is a way of thinking. It is a way of *being* in life…at work, at home, wherever you are.

It reflects a confidence that you have the capability and freedom to learn anything—a freedom to apply what you learn, to create something new in any moment.

It is a freedom to become. Even more, it is a permission and willingness to reach, increasing your ability to give.

Vital people don't blame; they find a way to participate more. They collaborate more, share more, create more. Vital people consider options, look for alternatives, and help other people see alternatives. Vital people look for ways to evolve their perspective about where they are and what they are doing rather than complain that others won't "let them" do anything new.

Vital people want the best for themselves and find a way to share that best. They share the best around them to create "better" for others—for individuals, teams, organizations, companies, and country.

Vital people see more, not less. Vital people learn to listen, and listen well, so they can understand more, communicate more, and collaborate more because it is interesting, fulfilling, and fun. It is joining the creative energy of life that makes life expand, not sitting silent, unmoving, and stagnant.

Vital people can be both leaders and followers. They can work with leaders at the top and people at the bottom equally well. They are present to the needs of the moment. They are willing to be open to possibilities and participate to their fullest in the moment knowing the moment is only part of a larger whole in which they live.

Vital people learn quickly that the habitual language in their head is only one of many possibilities. They know that being fixed on one idea or way of doing things causes hardship—for themselves and everyone around them. They know that Vitality is listening to, working with, and evolving ideas.

They know that becoming a Vital thinking person is becoming a fluid person who not only goes with the flow but is willing to take a new route, to learn new things and new ways of being that create greater freedom for themselves and the people around them.

Do you want that? Would you rather have employees like that or employees who have done the same things for years because that is all they were allowed to do?

When the market changes rapidly, you need employees you can train and who will work with you to help find the best way to get the job done. When you need employees who will exercise personal initiative, do you look for people who have only one view of your organization, or employees who have a broad understanding of it? People who feel encouraged and respected for stepping out and applying themselves to something new or people who are numb to possibilities?

We are talking about building a full powerhouse of Vital employees.

"Success is a fusion of company potential and employee potential."

— DR. JAMES A. ROBERTSON

The concept of Vitalized employees is embraced by progressive-thinking companies such as Google and Intel. We need these companies. We need their examples. We respect and admire them. But with the ever-increasing confusion and complexity in the world, we must also learn from them and share what we can to create ever greater strength and clarity in our own actions. We need to go beyond what they have accomplished. This is Vitality!

What are the key elements to becoming a Vital company with Vitalized employees? Does Vital mean creating more and more outsource channels so you can enlist more and more cost-effective employees? No. That would only dilute the inherent wisdom and morale of your current employees. Outsourcing to people who have little or no experience in your company, and often not even in your industry, will only place you further behind.

It *does* mean being willing to look at your organization and the history of managing that organization to find stagnation—where it begins, where it is hiding, how it is growing…and stop it!

It means being willing to lead in a different way—by example, with a clear continual flow of communication across the organization, both vertically and horizontally. It means instilling a strong foundation of basic common skills that starts moving sludge of stagnation and creates a flow of interactivity that inhibits stagnation's growth.

It means creating continual personal development goals for individual employees and team participation. Creating "reach goals" associated with "what's in it for me" generates interest, spurs learning, and develops Vitality.

It means instilling core skills across the organization that develop quality communication and collaboration, recognized and practiced by every employee in every function at every level. Let's take that a step further: It means instilling foundational skills that are recognized, expected, respected, and requested of every employee at every level throughout your organization.

It means accepting that employee stagnation has been the norm in your organization for a long time, but it is no longer acceptable. It means recognizing that "busy" doesn't mean Vital. It means identifying and clarifying locations and practices that make employees stagnant and disinterested…and changing them.

It means creating a new enhanced Vision and Mission to be a leader in reaching, tapping into, and leveraging employee potential as your key asset. It means focusing on skills, practices, incentives, and rewards designed to nurture, encourage, and partner with your employees to recognize and expand their potential—every day.

It means connecting with your employees' innate need for confidence and personal internal assurance that they can support their families and contribute to their communities in a better way all the time—by working for you.

This is why I am here, writing this book. Evolving the human potential in your organization is not an option; it is an imperative. The landscape of our leadership thinking must change if we are to become Vital, flexible businesses and organizations capable of withstanding rapid change. We must develop our core asset of employee potential to step up to the challenge of chaos and the confusion of complexity, while continuing to attract quality customers, investors, and top talent.

Even the attraction of top talent has to change. The driving requirement for top talent is no longer just to be a degreed specialist. Top talent now must also demonstrate proven people-leadership skills in enhancing employee potential in every function and every level. And boundaries for negative behavior must change. Sharpen your focus on Vitality!

This book's intention is to help you understand the depth, breadth, and challenges of the stagnation crisis. We will help you take the first step by providing new foundational programs for employees and leadership that you can employ right now to start overcoming stagnation of thought and action, and create a new competitive energy for the company.

The problem is over a hundred years in the making, and it won't be solved overnight. But it won't be solved at all unless you take the first step to change your perspective as a leader—a leader of extraordinary human potential, not just numbers.

Vitalize Your Workforce provides new ways of thinking about employee stagnation, and new leadership paradigms to lead and maintain Vitalization. Finally, you can measure and understand the depth of employee stagnation anywhere in your organization—before, during, and after implementing our Vitality. Leadership and Employee Vitalization Programs. I will work with you to help define, prioritize, and customize the key elements of your Vitalization initiative and help keep it on track.

As part of your Vitalization initiative, I will introduce leadership programs that will gain employee attention and interest in your new vision for the company. And I will introduce new foundational employee programs that effectively start clearing the debilitating sludge of employee stagnation and instilling a sense of personal employee responsibility and opportunity—reaching for their own future while working for you.

CHAPTER 2
SUMMARY

*"Success is a fusion of company potential
and employee potential."*

— DR. JAMES A. ROBERTSON

VITALITY IS NOT AN ADJECTIVE OR AN ADVERB. IT IS A WAY of thinking. It is a way of *being* in life…at work, at home, wherever you are. It is a confidence that you have the capability and freedom to learn anything—a freedom to apply what you learn, to create something new in any moment. It is a freedom to become. Even more, it is a permission and willingness to reach, increasing your ability to give.

The concept of vitalized employees is embraced by progressive thinking companies such as Google and Intel. We need these companies. We need their examples. We respect and admire them. But with the ever-increasing confusion and complexity in the world, we must also learn from them and share what we can to create ever greater strength and clarity for our own actions. We need to go beyond what they have accomplished. This is Vitality!

Leading for Vitality means being willing to lead in a different way—by example, with a clear continual flow of communication across the organization, both vertically and horizontally. It means instilling a strong foundation of basic common skills that starts to clear the sludge of stagnation, creating a flow of interactivity that inhibits stagnation's growth.

Vitalize Your Workforce is here to provide a new way to measure the depth and breadth of stagnation in your organization, help you embed new Vitality Leadership concepts and accountabilities, and reach employees with new sustainable programs designed to continually release the sludge of personal stagnation, while sparking personal initiative, interest, and loyalty. And that is just the start!

NOTES

Actions: _____

_____

_____

_____

_____

Call Whom: _____

_____

_____

_____

_____

By When: _____

_____

_____

_____

_____

"You can't manage what you can't measure."

— PETER DRUCKER

CHAPTER 3

REAL CHANGE REQUIRES MEASUREMENT

By Dr. James A. Robertson

PETER DRUCKER HIGHLIGHTED A FUNDAMENTAL PRINCIPAL of management: *"You can't manage what you can't measure,"* referring to generating and using hard data to help make critical decisions. Since then, the market shifted from an industrial to information focus, then shifted from information to information ubiquity in the 2010s. The market is now accelerating into the 2020s with advanced automation and the need not just to use the people in our charge but to harness the potential of our human assets for greater and more flexible contribution.

This need is multidimensional. Organizations must recognize there *is* hidden potential in all of their employees that they must harness or lose. Leaders must identify and implement programs that will touch, awaken, and evolve the potential of their employees into proactive, measurable action. Of critical importance is the recognition that leaders must also evolve their own habitual management thinking and practices of leading employees. This evolution can be challenging and sometimes painful, requiring new measurements, new perspectives about employees, new leadership skills, and new incentives.

One of the cornerstones of the Vitalize Your Workforce approach is the ability to measure the "soft issues" around employee potential, and management's ability to recognize, enhance, and apply that potential. To this end, Vitalize Your Workforce focuses on establishing a new baseline of measuring tools and capabilities that include measuring the levels of Stagnation and Vitalization in organizations in a way that allows these critical parameters to be managed at both the individual and organizational levels.

The power of measurement of "soft issues" is exemplified by the following case study:

CASE STUDY

MEASUREMENT RESOLVES DISCORDANT COMMUNICATION AMONG C-LEVELS

While working with IBM Consulting Group, I was contracted to help develop a Strategic Plan for a division of the government. The new chief director, a man in his thirties with a doctoral degree, represented a new administration. He was much younger than the five reporting department heads who were all in their fifties. The chief director found himself in conflict with the department heads and seemed to be at an impasse at a critical time for decisions.

Situation

As was my usual practice, I started the resolution process with one-on-one interviews with the chief director and each department head who would be participating in the strategic planning workshop.

In my opening interview with the chief director, he said, "I have had enough. This is an age issue; they are out to get me—we have meetings, we agree what needs to be done, and they go off and do exactly the opposite. If they do not change their attitude, I am going to fire the lot of them!" I then interviewed each of the five department heads, and each said roughly the same thing, "I have had enough. This is an age issue; he is out to get us—we have meetings, agree what needs to be done, we do what we have agreed, and at the next meeting, he tears us apart. If he does not change his attitude, we are going to resign en masse!" There was tension everywhere.

A few days later, we all met in the strategic planning workshop. Tension was obvious and the progress slow. The delegates oozed distrust and resentment. I applied my proprietary StratSnap© Strategic Process,[11] which is a concise and highly effective technique for quickly and effectively arriving at high-value prioritized ratings related to any significant business issue.

As usually happens, we had no difficulty synthesizing the Seven Critical Concerns with regard to strategic issues in the department. The process involved the participants brainstorming about their concerns as a group, then each separately formulating their Seven Critical Concerns. The individual Critical Concerns were then combined in a collaborative process that ensured all voices in the room were heard and that their thoughts were collated in an inclusive manner. The result of this session was a high level of buy-in regarding to the Top Seven Critical Factors for this department.

The next stage in the process was for delegates to weight privately the seven factors in terms of relative importance, adding to a total of 100 percent. The delegates returned their rating sheets. I captured the results privately and displayed the end result to all concerned.

The essence of the results is presented in this chart:

Serial	Factors	CDir	Dir1	Dir2	Dir3	Dir4	Dir 5
1	Critical Concern 1	30	3	3	3	3	3
2	Critical Concern 2	24	5	5	5	5	5
3	Critical Concern 3	18	8	8	8	8	8
4	Critical Concern 4	12	12	12	12	12	12
5	Critical Concern 5	8	18	18	18	18	18
6	Critical Concern 6	5	24	24	24	24	24
7	Critical Concern 7	3	30	30	30	30	30
	Total	**100**	**100**	**100**	**100**	**100**	**100**

The chief director allocated a weight of around 30 percent to the factor that he regarded as most important and around 3 percent to the factor he regarded as least important. The department heads allocated very high weights to the factor the chief director regarded as incidental, and very low weights to the factor he regarded as critical. The comparison was stark.

I reconvened the session, displayed the results, and shared my conclusion with the delegates. There was complete agreement with regard to the department's critical priorities. The problem lay with the interpretation of those factors' relative importance. Simply put, in meetings the five department heads readily agreed on what was important, but that was where the agreement ended. Once they left the meeting, the directors would all devote the bulk of their time, resources, and creativity to those areas they regarded as critical and would ignore the things they regarded as incidental, which happened to be the chief director's critical priorities. This difference was *not* due to a malevolent agenda but simply a consequence of different priorities.

I presented my conclusion and suggested that since there was a new administration with new priorities, the directors should simply choose to align themselves with the chief director's priorities. There was immediate understanding of the problem and acceptance of the resolution by everyone in the room.

The next morning, the contrast and excitement were palpable; the team reconvened, and all continued to agree with my diagnosis. There were smiles all around and animated conversation as people compared notes and recounted the exciting observations they had made. The problem was solved; the department heads agreed to realign themselves with the priorities of the chief director, and they committed themselves afresh to working constructively and collaboratively with him.

Value

This case study exemplifies one of the techniques elemental to the Vitalize Your Workforce program, demonstrating the power of reducing soft and apparently intangible situations to numeric measures.

The Vitalize Your Workforce program uses various techniques to develop numeric measures with regard to diverse elements of our facilitative work. These include:

- Critical Concerns Process[12] with regard to vitality of the workforce
- Critical Objectives[13] with regard to workforce vitality
- Stagnation-Vitalization rating for the Organization as a whole—
  a survey that uses a set of carefully crafted key phrases to highlight the Stagnation State versus the Vitalized State of the Organization
- Stagnation-Vitalization rating of Organization Elements
  or Business Units—the components of the organization
- Stagnation-Vitalization rating of individual employees—
  a key word response survey that evaluates the level of Stagnation or

Vitalization of individuals and generates reports in similar format to the Organization Element assessment

These various measurements translate the domain of workforce Stagnation-Vitalization into a quantified state that is amenable to rigorous analysis to ensure a high-value business outcome from Vitalize Your Workforce initiatives.

We regard the measurement of these so-called "intangibles" as a critical component of an effective business solution. This sets a new baseline for considering and managing employee evolution from being Stagnant to a new Vitality that is both concrete and visible.

CHAPTER 3
SUMMARY

IT IS WIDELY BELIEVED THAT RESOLVING ISSUES SUCH AS Stagnation is a hit or miss affair, based on "gut feel" and "intuition." This is not the case. With properly designed survey instruments and facilitation techniques, such as the Vitalize Your Workforce assessment tools and the StratSnap© strategic facilitation technique,[14] it is entirely possible to develop reliable numeric measures of performance, objectives, and new development criteria.

Chapter 3 elucidates this thinking by presenting a case study in which the use of numeric measures rapidly defused a highly toxic case of misaligned priorities in a manner that brought about a dramatic change in emphasis and perspective as well as fundamental realignment of priorities.

NOTES

Actions: _____

_____

_____

_____

_____

Call Whom: _____

_____

_____

_____

_____

By When: _____

_____

_____

_____

_____

"We cannot solve our problems with the same level of thinking that created them."

— ALBERT EINSTEIN

SECTION 2
VITALIZE ISSUE RESOLUTION AND PROBLEM SOLVING

"Leadership is solving problems. The day soldiers stop bringing their problems is the day you have stopped leading them. They have either lost confidence that you can help or concluded you do not care. Either case is a failure in leadership."

– COLIN POWELL

CHAPTER 4

PROBLEM SOLVING IS A PROBLEM

LEADERSHIP IS SOLVING PROBLEMS, IN EVERY FUNCTION AND at every level of an organization. The failure of leaders to solve problems at every level stops vitality in its tracks. Lack of problem-solving emphasis within an organization disintegrates interest and trust in the leadership, and erodes willingness to work hard. It diminishes the value of goal setting and the emphasis on teamwork, communication, and achievement. Simply stated: Your employees can't work to their potential or yours if their problems are not solved quickly and well.

Unfortunately, the pandemic lack of emphasis on problem solving is often silent. Unsolved problems do not sound an alarm until the problem becomes so great that it impedes action or intended outcomes. The resulting cost and effort to restore the smooth interworking of a function or relationship can be lengthy and extensive.

The importance of continual and effective problem solving is paramount. Effective evolution of your business requires looking far beyond just being resilient—looking beyond just returning to where you were before. It requires intentionally extending your vision to where you want to be and encouraging employees on every level to identify existing problems as well as emerging problems and be proactive in helping resolve them, every day.

Two of the silent yet pervasive causes for lack of issue resolution and problem solving are:

- Employee deference to "someone above me who has the responsibility for solving that problem," (i.e., "It's not my job," or worse, "I am not approved to help—no one will listen to me." And even worse, "My manager doesn't care. He/she never solves any problems, so why should I try?").

- Managers and employees having little or no understanding of or training in how to think about resolving issues and problems so that:
  - ▸ everyone involved can understand them
  - ▸ the solution benefits everyone involved
  - ▸ the process increases proactive interest in problem solving

In this chapter, I will provide four very different situations that exemplify problems and issues to be resolved, why they were not resolved, and the high value gained by their resolution. If you are aware of similar situations anywhere in your organization, you have stagnation. Each situation has ramifications for your organization that are intolerable in an accelerating world. The three primary words to keep in mind are: People, Process, and Perspective. If you are ignoring any of these, you can't have Vitality in your organization.

CASE STUDY

JOHN: A TRUE PROBLEM SOLVER[15]

John is a tall, broad-shouldered African-American man with a smile that wraps all the way around his head. He leads a day shift on the production line of heavy metal products at a prominent truck axle manufacturing plant.

Though he has little formal education, John radiates natural leadership skills and a positive can-do energy. It is easy to see that he is calm, confident, aware, and open to new ideas.

As a team leader of a production line, John struggled with continual conflict between the day shift and the night shift. Employee complaining and negativity centered on three issues: new materials stored incorrectly, production lines left cluttered for the next run, and tools left in unsafe locations. Both the day- and night-shift teams had tough, negative attitudes, with no end in sight.

John worked hard to get to know each of the line members on both shifts. He participated in the work, recognized effort, bought pizzas for lunch, and even volunteered to install a new kitchen for a man on the night shift in hopes that his generosity would soften the man to become more of a team player. Unfortunately, his efforts brought about little change.

Looking for a solution, John reached out and learned the Vitalize Issue Resolution Process. This process introduced John to the idea of increasing his team's understanding of the importance of their work by sharing the company's Vision and Mission, and how their department fit into the larger scheme of things, in a way they could understand and internalize.

John engaged each man individually to define all the issues he could think of. Then, he gradually gathered them together to talk about what was working and what was not. He took notes about their complaints and ideas, displaying them on an easel, so they could visualize their input. The men soon realized that someone was actually listening to their complaints and ideas. They started to believe their input had value. Slowly, their resistance melted.

John knew their language. He knew their expertise was production, not classroom learning. But more importantly, he knew they could help design a new way of getting the job done, if asked the right way.

He met with the day- and night-shift teams separately so they could relax and feel free to chat. Then, John combined the lists of issues and suggestions. He shared them with everyone as one group over donuts and coffee.

Some men were curious about what others had shared, some were barely tolerant, and others remained resistant. John's leadership picked up steam as he spoke. They could feel it.

John slowly and respectfully went over all of the issues with each person individually, letting the men gripe and add issues as they went along. He then offered a production wager: "I'll bet if we could find a way to move this, straighten this, and do this, we could double our weekly output and have time left over."

Some of the men grunted their habitual response, "It will never happen." John's team clearly saw him as a caring, participating leader, but they didn't see how John's ideas applied to them. It was a "John versus all the rest" situation. "No one has ever cared" and "What's in it for me?"

thinking was prevalent, making it difficult to introduce new ideas and "possibility thinking."

Their perspective was, "Management does not care about me or recognize me as an individual, so why should I care?" And critically, "Nothing ever changes, so why bother?" How sad.

So John changed the game. He adopted the Vitalize Issue Resolution and Problem-Solving Process that provides a clear, systematic way for all employees to share respectful communication and problem solving at any level, in any function, any time.

John said, "Wait a minute. Let's find out." He then turned the page and drew a diagram of the shop floor with the delivery doors, the rail track in the floor, the hoist track overhead, and the loading dock. Now he was speaking their language. They could visually see what he was talking about, and suddenly, they became engaged.

Because his team thought and spoke visually, John drew their thoughts in simple process flows on a chalkboard. Then he drew simple diagrams representing their known issues and their recommended solutions so everyone could see, understand, and have some common basis for agreement. He spoke and drew their language.

John then gave his team permission to think about how the entire end-to-end flow could work better. He said there were some things that couldn't change, such as the location and direction of the railway tracks for incoming materials, but the rest of the process was open for improvement.

Problem Solvers Generate Vitality!

As ideas and suggestions began to flow, John drew the recommended changes on the board as 1) proof that someone was actually listening, and 2) proof that someone was listening well. They then physically walked through their own solutions, making the practicalities and possibilities for change even more real. John knew that if he could convince his team that the changes they wanted really were possible, their enthusiasm for new solutions would grow into implementation of new systems that would reap high rewards.

John took small, sequential steps to expand his team members' perspectives. He walked his people outside the building to show them how their incoming steel was delivered. They walked inside through other locations in the building so they could understand the history and reasons for their current shop floor layout. He then introduced his team to the people in the department that receives their finished truck axle parts.

Here they learned how the parts were being used, and what would make the finished assembly job easier.

Communication and collaboration gained momentum daily, resulting in a formal recommendation provided to management that included people, process, perspective, and *profit*! John's new problem-solving team:

- identified and designed a new entrance for incoming material
- added overhead hangers to facilitate swift placement for manufacturing
- created a new door designated for removal of shop floor residue
- added a line-timing system that would help maintain a workable rhythm for their hands-on work
- added rest intervals and rest locations to increase focus and production
- added a labeling and time-marking station to address production challenges

The result? John and his team more than doubled their volume with less stress. They now meet once a month to continue issue identification and resolution.

The company recognized John and his men as an exemplary team for their vision and teamwork. Every man received a commendation for his participation. This commendation might have been the first-ever in their lives, and it had significant value for the men at work, at home, and in their communities. Since then, confidence is up. Self-esteem is up. Attitude and loyalty are up, and production is up.

John is a proactive, natural leader, respected by management and valued by his men. He is Vitalizing every aspect of the business in his charge every day and encouraging his team to do the same and more. Give your natural people-leaders permission and the right tools and watch what happens!

Problem Solvers Help Communicate

Communication from the top needs to be translated at every level and into the language pertinent for each function so every employee understands and personally connects with what you have to say. Finding and mentoring your natural people-leaders is the key to managing this communication.

There are natural people-leaders throughout your organization on every level, in each function, who know the language of their function. They may not have advanced degrees, or even a college education, but they are people who are generally recognized and admired by employees in that function—people who are ready and willing to step up and help lead new initiatives or resolve issues if you give them a chance. Natural people-leaders can engage employees in a function or group to identify and define issues, clarify what is important to the participants, think about possible alternatives for issue resolution, create and test new ideas or working models, and learn how employees would like to be recognized for their participation.

These natural people-leaders are a valuable part of your new communication team. You can mentor them for effective communication horizontally across a department and between departments, and you can easily expand their perspective and natural value to you by including them in your vertical communications.

> *"Your natural people-leaders are*
> *the hidden gems in your organization.*
> *Find them, mentor them, and recognize them.*
> *You'll be glad you did!"*

When your employees, natural people-leaders, and their peers learn a common-approved issue resolution and problem-solving process, and have permission and encouragement to identify and solve problems, employees don't have to wait for someone "authorized" to solve a problem, or hope that someone will care. They can start solving a problem right where they are, know how to communicate, form teams, explore alternatives, and gain attention for their observations and recommendations.

Another key aspect of Vitalizing your workforce is continually expanding your employees' perspectives about their jobs and your organization. This is an invaluable pursuit. Every job has an average of five adjacent functions that relate to it in some way. If employees don't know the source of their incoming work, or where it goes after they do their part, how do they know the value of their jobs and where they fit into the scheme of things? How do they identify and resolve problems impeding their performances? The answer is—they don't know their value, and they can't solve their own problems of performance.

Are these employees dumb? No. Are they capable of solving the problem? Probably. But their lack of perspective, training, and permission to solve problems any time anywhere is painfully lacking. How frustrated and Stagnant are these employees? Very.

When they are taught a quality issue-resolution and problem-solving process, when they are introduced to the people in the functions related to their job, and when they are given permission to communicate and collaborate for the betterment of everyone, and can interact with people-leaders, Vitality shines!

Vitalizing Your Workforce starts at the top. Vitalizing your vision, mission, culture, and policies to lead and support a progressive thinking, learning organization is an imperative. The Vitalize Your Workforce team understands that this refining process can take time and may surface conflict of vision among senior leaders. Our Strategic Snapshot (StratSnap) service quickly establishes the core strategic view of the problem and defines the solution.

CHAPTER 4
SUMMARY

LEADERSHIP IS SOLVING PROBLEMS—IN EVERY FUNCTION, on every level, every day. The failure of leaders to solve problems as soon as possible stops vitality in its tracks and causes stagnation.

The pandemic lack of problem solving is often silent, hidden until a major issue surfaces; then it is too late. Continuity of performance is interrupted while individuals, and often teams of individuals, try to determine the problem's source and extent, and work to resolve it. This extra effort steals time away from current jobs, often requires expensive overtime, and thwarts momentum.

To establish quality issue resolution and problem solving as a priority across the organization, the initiative must be implemented in every function and at every level, encouraging employees to take responsibility wherever they are. Require that all managers be trained in managing and mentoring vital problem-solving skills as critical criteria for hiring and promotion. If managers are not proactive in encouraging and mentoring problem solving for their employees, then their effectiveness in any people-leadership position is in question. Are they contributing to Stagnation or helping to dissolve stagnation and leading their teams to Vitality?

NOTES

Actions: _____
_____
_____
_____
_____

Call Whom: _____
_____
_____
_____
_____

By When: _____
_____
_____
_____
_____

"Without continual growth and progress, such words as improvement, achievement, and success have no meaning."

— BENJAMIN FRANKLIN

CHAPTER 5

PEOPLE PROBLEMS MAY BE PROCESS PROBLEMS–LOOK DEEPER!

CASE STUDY
MEDICAL OFFICE

Medical offices require the processing of extraordinary amounts of paperwork—personal records, treatment records, referral records, insurance records, etc. The steady stream of patients requiring support every day requires the staff to work under constant pressure to produce and review account data while maintaining an organized office and minimizing patient wait time.

*"Process problems soon produce
people problems."*

Any slowdown in the process creates annoyance for the patient. Over time, this turns into negativity, resentment, sometimes anger, and often slander among the office staff too. The physicians in the large office I'll be discussing below either didn't notice, didn't care, or in truth, didn't feel it was their problem—until patient complaints started coming in and appointment bookings began to decline.

Process problems and people problems require patience and a keen intention to identify and resolve the core problems rather than just treating surface personality issues. Issue resolution and problem solving are learned skills. They require someone willing to lead by asking questions, listening carefully, encouraging development of solutions and negotiating the best result for all.

None of the doctors in this office felt qualified or wanted to get into the middle of the office issues, but they knew the problems needed to be resolved. They asked for volunteers from the staff to lead the initiative. Knowing that the lead staff manager was part of the problem, the doctors suggested the resolution team be comprised of general staff members who were closer to the issues that required attention.

Four employees who consistently exhibited excellent people skills volunteered to work together as a problem-solving team. None of them had full college degrees, yet their natural people skills enabled them to move and work well throughout the office.

To start, they asked all eighteen employees to submit their complaints and issues anonymously on slips of paper. The team sorted and grouped the complaints to understand which grievances had the most negative impact on the office's functioning and working environment. Prioritizing the grievances helped them see the primary issues, with surprising results.

Some issues reported were: The reception desk chairs and file cabinets were too close together, creating difficulty in moving around the office and opening the files. Short employees couldn't reach the top file drawers, and stepping stools created more confusion. The early evening schedule for the cleaning company interrupted the employees' end-of-day workflow, and the cleaning crew was in the office for too long. Other issues included that the filing system was old, it could not easily accommodate new doctors or patients, and many files were difficult to read.

Once the team members organized these grievances, they shared their findings in a small staff meeting to encourage people to participate. The team recorded any other issues that emerged through the course of the discussion without judgment. As leaders, they kept a clear focus on finding resolutions.

The team members combined their thoughts into a recommendation they reviewed with all the staff to help confirm that their ideas were, in fact, heard and recorded correctly. The next step was to share their findings with the head of the office, a proactive decision-maker. The final recommendation included:

- converting the patient care office closest to the reception desk into a dedicated file room, with good lighting
- moving all files away from the reception area
- investigating new file cabinet designs with fewer high and low drawers, and possibly an electronic open and close capability to help with the weight
- providing a dedicated worktable and computer workspace
- changing the cleaning company's schedule
- updating the file folder design to provide "quick glance" information
- introducing movable hanging file folder carriers with wheels to hold finished and unfinished files in alphabetical order, so the tables and desks could be clear for the next shift
- investigating the introduction of an automated file search capability to accelerate the location and filing of patient and other records

The team members identified which recommendations they could act on right away and which were long-range solutions. Decisions were made and they were on their way.

The result? Both patients and employees liked the new office layout. It produced a calmer, happier office atmosphere where quicker records processing reduced overtime, thereby reducing operating costs. These monies were then channeled to a new fund for staff education. The new file cabinets and automation reduced physical stress, and the cleaning people worked on a new early morning schedule, eliminating customer service interference. The office environment and staff now represented a happy, respectful business, inside and out. The team's problem-solving results were a win-win for everyone.

The keys?

- Teaching and implementing a clear problem-solving practice for all employees in the organization.

- Encouraging their natural people-leaders to step forward and guide the problem-solving conversations, regardless of their level of formal education or position.
- Expanding employee perspective about the office—how it works, the variety of functions it supports, and the roles and responsibilities of each of the functions.
- Creating valuable opportunities and options for expanding employee job perspectives. The alternatives were unlimited, from internships in other departments or functions to permission to attend relevant association meetings.

Offering these options as a reward for continuing issue resolution and problem solving Vitalizes employees, expands perspective and confidence, and accelerates participation and creative thinking. That is Vitality!

CHAPTER 5
SUMMARY

"Process problems soon produce people problems."

NEGATIVITY AND COMPLAINING ARE PERVASIVE IN ANY organization, and in many organizations, they are getting worse. This is evidenced by companies experiencing higher and higher unwanted and unplanned employee turnover. That is, they are losing a lot of very good employees due to the negativity caused by lack of problem solving. In many cases, what sounds and looks like a personal problem may, in fact, be an unaddressed process problem.

When processes are up to date and run smoothly, work can be enjoyable and even fun. However, when there is any slowdown, repeated miscommunication, missing of deliverable dates, or customer frustration, employees rightly become annoyed. Not knowing the cause of the problem, employees often start blaming someone else along the line for the poor delivery. Or if there is questionable product quality and no overt management effort to rectify the problem, employees feel it reflects on them, and in many cases, it does, whether it is their fault or not. Over time, their frustration turns into negativity, resentment, anger, and often slander.

Hundreds of examples exist of process issues creating employee problems. Process and people problems require patience and keen attention to identify and resolve the core issue rather than just reacting to the resulting symptom of negativity.

Quality issue resolution requires implementing a clear, easily understood problem-solving process across an organization so employees learn and utilize a common problem-solving language and basic procedures to:

- understand what data is important to the office manager and doctor
- identify a problem in a way others can understand it
- analyze the problem's impact on the individuals, in-office teams, and the entire business
- develop alternative solutions and recommendations in a way the employees are easily recognized by the supervising manager

Implementing a foundational problem-solving process enables all employees to learn what is important to: 1) the organization, 2) the department, and 3) their specific manager. A foundational problem-solving process maintains a standard process for thinking and communicating at any level, and it supports problem-solving initiatives by natural people-leaders. It also facilitates the addition of function-specific problem-solving requirements such as those required for R&D or shipping, while maintaining the business-related guidelines for clear communication.

Additionally, continual expansion of employees' perspectives about 1) their job, 2) the adjacent function(s) related to their job, and 3) the rest of the organization, also infuses employee Vitality. Continually expanding employee perspectives instills a feeling of belonging to something greater than just their current job, enables greater communication, and encourages greater collaboration with adjacent departments to learn and solve problems as they arise.

NOTES

Actions: _____
_____
_____
_____
_____

Call Whom: _____
_____
_____
_____
_____
_____

By When: _____
_____
_____
_____
_____
_____

*"The art of communication
is the language of leadership."*

— JAMES HUMES

CHAPTER 6

VITALIZING VERTICAL AND HORIZONTAL COMMUNICATION

CASE STUDY
SUPPLY CHAIN PROBLEM[16]

Supply chains require thousands of communications, merged schedules, synchronized handoffs, and a steady stream of confirmations. Supply chains need constant attention. If data requirements change for one department and other departments don't get the memo, the result can close your doors.

A major US optical networks supplier released a new communications product line that required specialized installation techniques. The supplier expected the first orders to come from US-based customers with expertly trained installation crews who knew how to install and adapt advanced technologies. International orders were not expected in the first year, hence defining international installation requirements was not a priority.

To their surprise, US-based customers were not the first to order the new line. Newly emerging international companies around the world signed multi-billion-dollar orders for the new product almost immediately. These companies were just emerging into the international telecommunications arena. They had little or no experience installing, maintaining, or operating communications networks in their countries. To gain competitive advantage, they contracted these services from the US supplier, expecting high quality US-style support with a guaranteed service start-up date. The goal was early revenue to help cover the investment cost.

Overnight, the US firm was in trouble. It was not prepared. Its sales and negotiating team had assessed and priced the installation requirements "the way we have always done it," based on similar orders in other locations. The international installers not yet trained in the new product line showed up in various global locations with incorrect tools and incorrect documentation. Every day, the financial drain grew worse and worse. Dissatisfied customers threatened to cancel contracts, and they rightfully charged huge penalties for non-performance.

Rectifying the situation involved thousands of overtime hours and the loss of millions of dollars. What was the issue? A disconnect of communication across all the interrelated functions, from R&D to marketing, sales, bid and proposal, to supply chain, training, and maintenance.

Saudi Arabia signed a multi-billion-dollar contract based on a US "business as usual" estimate. Once there, the installation team, poised to lay the primary cable three meters underground—as required to meet health and safety regulations—quickly discovered solid bedrock beneath a relatively shallow layer of sand. This finding quickly negated all projected timelines and required a complete redesign of the product line for that country. The repair and service team then found that due to customs regulations for that country, it was financially and tactically impossible to establish an in-country repair and service function. New plans required development of a repair center in Egypt to serve Saudi's in-field service needs efficiently.

The problem was complex, multilayered, and immediate, with an imperative to solve it or lose the business. The emphasis on people, process, and perspective was magnified a thousand times in the initial chaos to resolve the problems, create new capabilities, and save the business.

To address the problems, the company enlisted problem-solving teams from each department involved in the project. Together, they reviewed every step from R&D to product development, sales, service, distribution, training, installation, supply chain, and maintenance. They learned about each other's departmental expertise, requirements, strengths, weaknesses, and fears. Most people had never met before since their previous culture had limited their focus to a particular job. They quickly learned to ask questions—why, what, how, and who—and share what they knew…*fast!*

Together, they defined new information flows connecting key departments. They established a new quality verification system to ensure timely transfer of new product installation and maintenance requirements to all departments involved in the sale, especially contracting and on-time installation and maintenance. The result was a 94 percent improvement in successful installations, an 80 percent increased customer satisfaction in 18 months, and 93 percent customer retention.

This evolution to rapid issue resolution took long hours and dedication across departments, functions, and even countries. The supplier did have to pay millions in poor performance penalties, but with consistent focus on high-quality issue resolution and problem-solving, it established a new sustainable platform for successful service.

Today, issue identification and problem solving are primary skills required and taught throughout the organization as both a personal and organizational responsibility. Leadership for problem solving is recognized at every level in every function, and are rewarded with real opportunity for long-term career expansion. This company soon became one of the most respected optical network suppliers in the world.

The lesson? Don't rest where you are. Institute a Vitalize Issue-Resolution and Problem-Solving Program across your organization now.

CHAPTER 6
SUMMARY

SUPPLY CHAINS REQUIRE THOUSANDS OF COMMUNICATIONS, merged schedules, synchronized handoffs, and a steady stream of confirmations. Supply chains need constant attention. If data requirements change for one department and other departments don't get the memo, the result can close your doors.

Due to the complexity of the supply chain process in many organizations, any problems that occur are multifaceted and multilayered, with an immediate imperative to solve the problems or lose the business. The emphasis on all three critical areas of people, process, and perspective is magnified a thousand times in the initial chaos of the problem, requiring full attention of people and financial resources until it is resolved.

Progressive thinking and learning organizations require quality problem solving as a universal primary skill that is taught and practiced throughout the organization, as both a personal and organizational responsibility. Quality problem solving must become a key criterion in hiring and for any promotion considerations. Expertise in Vitalize Issue Resolution and Problem Solving provides a common language, and simple sequential process to serve as your starting point for greater and greater employee participation. Employee participation in problem solving can be accelerated when it is recognized and rewarded in any function on any level, regardless of the person's level of formal education.

The lesson? Don't rest where you are. Vitalize Your Workforce! Institute a Vitalize Issue-Resolution and Problem-Solving Program across your organization now.

NOTES

Actions: _____

_____

_____

_____

_____

Call Whom: _____

_____

_____

_____

_____

_____

By When: _____

_____

_____

_____

_____

*"Negativity is expensive.
It costs companies millions of dollars each year."*

— GARY TOPCHI

CHAPTER 7

MISSION CRITICAL! CONFRONT NEGATIVITY HEAD-ON!

COMPLAINING AND NEGATIVITY ARE HIGHLY DETRIMENTAL issues for any and every organization. They can be the result of process problems, lack of clear cultural policies governing corporate behavior, family problems, or just having a bad day. Whatever the cause, as soon as you see or hear complaining or negativity, follow it! Use the Vitalize Issue-Resolution and Problem-Solving techniques to determine the cause, identify alternative solutions, create a recommendation, and resolve it quickly.

- Companies lose an estimated $3 billion per year to the effects of negative attitudes and behaviors at work.[17]
- 25 percent of employees witness workplace incivility every day, and 50 percent say they are the direct targets of an uncivil act at least once a day.[18]
- The remainder of your employees (67 percent) are either disengaged (51 percent), doing only what they must do to maintain their jobs and collect their paychecks, or actively disengaged (16 percent), actively sabotaging what your handful of engaged employees are doing.[19]

Complainers can be loud and intrusive or subtle and remote. They can be in the same department or in another location. Wherever they are, complaining affects those expressing it and those hearing it. Stress increases and often leads to illness, absenteeism, and high, costly turnover.

> *"Complainers usually do not see themselves as negative people. They think of themselves as merely responding appropriately to annoying, aggravating, and unfortunate circumstances. What makes it so difficult to deal with chronic complainers is how resistant they are to support, cheering up, or advice."*
>
> — GUY WINCH, Ph.D. CLINICAL PSYCHOLOGY

Complaining is often habitual. It may be a learned trait from the family environment, or a poor defense to cover insecurity. It can show up as blame, resistance to change, or even sabotage.

> *"Complaining is contagious. It spreads like a virus among individuals, departments, customers, suppliers, and the Internet…essentially everywhere."*[20]

Addressing negativity and complaining is Mission Critical! It must be addressed as a major issue and managed openly, clearly, and directly.

Have you ever watched a group of people who enjoy working together or talking at lunch? They share a sense of lightness, spontaneity, and fun. Freedom and trust allow them to be expressive in a playful way since they feel safe in the moment.

Add a negative person into the mix. What happens? Spontaneity turns to hesitation. Conversation stops. People move away for their own protection. The situation becomes awkward for both the individual and the group. The next time people gather and the complainer approaches, the group disbands before the person reaches them.

As a leader, what happens to your focus and productivity when this occurs? Communication and teamwork decline, concentration and performance diminish, productivity lags, schedules slip, commitments go unsatisfied, and healthcare costs increase. Your ability to lead this organization becomes increasingly difficult.

> *"Negativity affects both employee and customer satisfaction."*

When a customer or employee problem becomes apparent, the tone and speed of the company response is the number one factor in influencing how much an employee or customer trusts a company. Any negativity in the environment or in the response directly affects the employee or customer's decision to leave and not return.

For instance, when patients come to a front desk, they may stand in line and observe the interactions of the attending staff for three to five minutes while signing in or simply waiting to ask a question. What happens when they hear, see, or feel the negativity and awkwardness within your staff?

Negativity and complaining are more pervasive than you would like to think. Only 4 percent of dissatisfied customers or employees ever voice a complaint.[21] Pay attention! If only 4 percent of unhappy people speak up, then how large is the actual problem? For every five people who complain, 130 remain silent.[22] This means that 91 percent of unhappy customers will not willingly do business with you again.[23] What are the top two reasons they don't want to work with you again?

- Poor customer or employee treatment
- Failure to solve a problem[24]

Why bring this to your attention? Because managers who are not people-leaders are a big part of your employee stagnation.

Managers who fail to resolve negative situations quickly lose employee respect and loyalty. Issues left unaddressed signal to employees that their manager (and hence the organization) does not care. This, in turn, magnifies that the employee's negativity is well founded and there is no use trying. Stagnant again. Why would employees want to work for a manager who fails to solve problems and check negative behavior? The answer is: They don't, and they eventually leave. Most of this turnover is unwanted and costly, directly affecting the bottom line.

Without a formal issue resolution process taught and implemented throughout an organization, neither the manager nor the employees have the power or authority to solve problems as they arise. The longer the issues stay active, the deeper the negative effect. This stalemate produces stagnation—over and over.

Why Managers Don't Take Action

The top seven reasons why managers fail to resolve complaining and negativity at work are (in no particular order):

- The situation is uncomfortable.

- There is no approved, unified problem-solving process in place.
- Addressing negativity is often regarded as "personal."
- No reward system exists for addressing negative situations.
- Negative situations are exhausting.
- No established boundaries exist to limit recurrence.
- Human Resources is seen as the default department responsible for addressing and resolving these situations, e.g., "it's not my problem."

No wonder so few leaders address complaining and negativity, and that even fewer achieve lasting results.

Until now, the only options for dealing with a difficult employee were to: a) counsel the person, b) increasingly isolate the person, c) change or diminish the person's job, or d) increase reasons to release the person with as few ramifications as possible. This process takes a long time and weakens everyone involved.

> *"We can no longer look the other way or delay correction.*
> *We must learn how to manage complaining and negativity*
> *in a new positive, progressive way."*

New Approach

Today we need to be proactive, specific, and provide new solutions. These solutions can easily include: establishing a progressive learning and opportunity reward program, enlisting employee choice to participate in their own future, and creating boundaries for negative behavior with clear guidelines.

When we activate the powerful paradigm of employee choice—choice to participate, not participate, and how much to participate in progressive work experience programs—choice links employee responsibility for their own career enhancement. It is no longer a one-way street.

This combination challenges habitual "welfare thinking" (only here for the benefits) and helps interrupt the common "What have you done for me lately?" complaint about the organization. Importantly, establishing employee choice, and tracking employee participation and personal initiative, helps you provide a natural mirror. It enables you to set new boundaries and guidelines to better manage negativity and complaining.

Add these elements to your Vitality Culture and Policy Guidelines so the opportunities and boundaries are clear.

The clarity facilitates communication, mentoring, and dialogue about employment retention. The choices are no longer nebulous, and the program is expandable and sustainable.

CHAPTER 7
SUMMARY

COMPLAINING AND NEGATIVITY ARE DETRIMENTAL TO every aspect of an organization. Internally, they spread like a virus, often silent yet pervasive, discouraging everyone in their paths. Externally, relationships with suppliers and affiliates become stressed and customers certainly sense negativity and go elsewhere.

How deep is that pain? A whopping 91 percent of unhappy customers will not willingly do business with you again. Employees feel the same way. The top reasons they don't want to work with an under-performing manager again are poor treatment and failure to solve a problem.

Whether negativity is learned at home, at school, or through the burdensome complaining and negativity purveyed in the news, leaders need to take focused, well-defined actions to curb negativity and procreate vitality throughout the organization.

Focused well-defined actions can include:

- Establishing a new paradigm program for continual progressive work experience(s) for employees, based on demonstrated personal initiative and participation.

- Activating the powerful paradigm of employee choice: choice to participate, not participate, and how much to participate in the progressive experience programs. Choice links employees' responsibility for their own career enhancement to the company provision of continual new opportunity.

- Adding these guidelines to your Vitality Culture and Policy Guidelines so they become elemental to marketing, hiring, promotion, and facilitating replacement of continually negative employees

NOTES

Actions: _____

_____

_____

_____

_____

Call Whom: _____

_____

_____

_____

_____

By When: _____

_____

_____

_____

_____

"A powerful process automatically takes care of progress, productivity and profits."

– AMIT KALANTRI

CHAPTER 8

EMBEDDING CRITICAL ISSUE RESOLUTION AND PROBLEM SOLVING

IN THE PREVIOUS CHAPTERS, WE PROVIDED EXAMPLES OF some pervasive issues and problems yet to be solved. These common problems manifest themselves differently in different organizations, but the reality is, if you want to create a sustainable Vitality culture with strong Vitality Leadership in your organization, these problems need continuous clear resolution.

The need for a common process became loud and clear in our dialogue with groups across the country. When asked what kind of problems they had in their jobs, the lists easily grew longer and longer. When asked whether problems were ever solved, the most common answer was "rarely." When asked about the effect of problems not being solved, the most common answer was: "We go back to our desks; nothing ever changes, so why try?"

Inquiring further to find the actual root of the problems not being resolved, the answer was again loud and clear. We asked whether anyone had ever been taught how to approach a problem, that is, how to think about problems in order to solve them? The answer was clearly no. Not in school, sometimes at home, and certainly not at work. A few of the seminar attendees shared that they did take a course or two "somewhere along the way" in general problem-solving, but they felt there was no way to apply what they learned at work. Either their supervisor was not interested in solving a problem or did not know how to solve it, or there was no leadership support, or no reward. In short, others did not share the same interest in solving a problem. This is what pervasive stagnation looks like.

As a result, all the employees could do was hope someone else would notice the problem and step in to help solve it. If they went around their supervisor, it might affect their jobs. If they did not, that would also affect their jobs, but at least they would have jobs. As a leader, is that what you want?

Suggestion Boxes and Open-Door Policies

To get deeper into the heart of the problem, the author spoke with more than 2,400 mid-range managers in fifteen states. The participants represented a wide variety of industries, including aerospace, medical, manufacturing, retail, education, information technology, Homeland Security, legal, housing, transportation, and more. Topics of discussion included diminishing employee involvement, employees' lack of interest and loyalty for their work and workplaces, and how leadership can assist in effectively and efficiently reducing complaining and negativity in the workplace.

We asked participants what processes their companies provided to resolve issues and problems. The general response was, "not many." The only specific examples they offered were the old ideas of:

- Open-door policies (for people to come and ask questions or talk about issues)
- Suggestion boxes
- Human Resources (HR) support

Approximately 64 percent of the participants (1,500 people) said they tried to practice an open-door policy, but they admitted it was largely ineffective. People could knock on the door at any time, and it was usually the same people who came to talk about the same problems. Their conversations rarely resolved anything. The employees felt welcomed and heard, but they were disappointed when the situation continued as before. They respected the manager as a person, but as a leader who effectively solved problems, their respect decreased more and more over time.

How did the manager feel? Frustrated. Almost 100 percent of managers said there was no effective method provided by the organization to manage negativity and complaining. They did not try to do more on their own because of possible of legal ramifications, fear of retribution, or possible negative marks on their own job report.

The "visiting" employee became a distraction to the manager over time, and an unproductive use of valuable time. This is a no-win situation for both the manager and the employee. Employee participation eventually declines while the manager's reputation also suffers. Both become discouraged and wonder whether trying to make things better is worth the effort. That's stagnation.

Asked whether they took advantage of suggestion boxes, less than 10 percent of survey participants even had suggestion boxes available. Asked whether they ever received a suggestion, these managers let out a low chuckle with a clear "no." The few who did receive suggestions didn't know what to do with them. No effective process was in place to elevate the issue for resolution or for them to make changes themselves.

This answer led us to ask: Why don't people use a suggestion box? What is missing? It's anonymous, safe, and available anywhere.

The answer: Employees never see anything happen with their suggestions, so why bother? It wouldn't matter anyway.

This led us to dig deeper: Why are suggestions rarely or never implemented? The answer was very practical and very real: Because most employees don't know *how* to write a suggestion so that someone else will read it, understand what it means, or care.

We then asked whether their organizations had a process to teach people how to write an effective suggestion, or to teach employees what is important to the company, or what is important to the department? Does the company teach its employees the important factors to consider when analyzing an issue and how to think about a solution?

An overwhelming 100 percent of the survey participants said, "no," their company had no such process. Further, they had never really thought about it. Consider this: If you don't teach employees how to think about what is important to the organization, how to think about a problem, or how to create a viable suggestion that managers and leaders will want to read, how can they offer a qualified, clear recommendation?

Then we asked managers: "Have you ever taken the time to let employees know how you think—what is important to you?" Again, the answer was a definite "no," 100 percent of the time. It was a completely new thought.

If an employee is going to write a suggestion that management will take seriously, the employee needs to know what to look for, what is important in analyzing a situation, and how to develop and offer alternative solutions. Without education on how to write (or verbally relate) a suggestion, most people won't try. This only leads to more silence, frustration, and personal stagnation.

Key point? Without a clear process for how to think about an issue and how best to offer a suggestion, employees feel stuck. The result?

- Avoidance of communication altogether
- Apathy about improving any difficult situation
- Resignation to leave things as they are and go home
- Discouragement about issue resolution and the organization
- More and more stagnation

If open-door policies and suggestion boxes don't work, what are the alternatives?

We asked survey participants whether they had any other method to resolve negativity and complaining. Only four out of 2,400 people surveyed (0.2 percent) had taken the initiative to develop their own methods for issue resolution. Their methods included facilitating open inquiry, identifying and collecting information on issues, identifying alternatives, and recommending the best solutions. They engaged employees in problem analysis, finding solutions, and making recommendations. The employees helped implement their own recommendations and received encouragement to identify more areas for improvement. Note: That was four out of 2,400.

> *"If 91 percent of your unhappy employees are unwilling to work with you again, how do you build a Vitalized, agile, and flexible workforce?"*

Some Pertinent Questions

If you asked anyone in your organization to define how to think about a problem, how to assess a problem for its scope and impact on the job, department, or business—could they? If you asked anyone to define a problem and its impact in a way that others can understand and care about it, could they? If you asked anyone to identify and assess alternative solutions to the problem in a way that includes information pertinent to the supervisor's thinking and pertinent to making decisions for the department or business, could they? If only a handful of people can, then you are inadvertently breeding stagnation in your company—everywhere.

Progressive thinking and learning organizations that are committed to creating an organization full of vitality view employee problem-solving skills as critical for everyone, at all levels.

Why establish formal issue resolution and problem-solving skill training as a requirement for all employees?

- Communication and collaboration thrive when there is a bond, something in common—a language, a view, a goal, or other recognizable element that enables employees to relate to each other.
- Learning the same issue resolution and problem-solving process (detail by function may change) enables employees to join or audit problem-solving dialogues anytime, anywhere.
- Auditing an active problem-solving session, whether in your own department or another (as at Google), is a readily available learning opportunity both to deepen the employee's understanding of your generic problem-solving process and continually expand the employee's perspective of the business. Whether participating or auditing, the employee gains confidence learning from others how to collaborate, lead, participate, research, analyze, and more without feeling threatened or challenged in their position.
- Employees move, jobs change, managers change, problems change. Designing and implementing a generic core process for your organization provides a consistent process that supersedes these changes in personnel. This core process and skill requirement becomes one of the important reliable "knowns" in the midst of continual change.
- Once the core process is defined, how the detail is addressed by function is adaptable.
- Recognizing employee personal initiative and participation in problem solving now becomes easy. You will you begin to identify your natural people-leaders; be able to link their overt leadership with new learning opportunities, exemplifying their positive behaviors; and include these natural people-leaders in your vertical and horizontal communications network.

A New Sustainable Approach

Organizations need a new sustainable approach to issue resolution and problem solving that clearly communicates it's a new day. The approach needs to be a simple, visible, replicable process that teaches, encourages, and rewards employees at all levels to become proactive in issue resolution and problem solving. When everyone is taught the same basic principles for solving problems, initiative rises and solution teams form anywhere, anytime, in any department or across departments.

The Vitalize Your Workforce (VYW) Issue Resolution and Problem-Solving Process starts with the basics that are elemental to problem solving in an enterprise. It includes: a simple step-by-step description of how to think about a problem, how to determine solution criteria that are important to a team or department, how to recommend alternative solutions, how to compare solutions, and how to forward a recommendation that is easily understood and considered by the receiver.

The simplicity of the sequence allows application across functions, enables customization of the language and data relevant to each function (marketing has different language and data criteria than shipping), facilitates communication and mentoring, and encourages participation in problem-solving sessions across departments.

The VYW Process helps leaders instill a sense of company-wide responsibility for identifying and solving problems, provides clear permission and encouragement for employee participation, provides a measurable system for employee opportunity reward, and sets a foundation for ROI.

CHAPTER 8
SUMMARY

THE IDEA OF ISSUE RESOLUTION AND PROBLEM SOLVING is so common that it is often overlooked, assumed as a "given," and often not declared as a core critical skill across the organization. From a leadership perspective, problem-solving may be regarded as a vertical responsibility for those charged with delivering financial results. This is true—it is.

But what about the rest of the organization? What about all the employees who have day-to-day responsibilities, who are conscientious, and in their hearts and minds do want to do a good job but can't because problems that affect their performance are not resolved. Are these problems inconsequential? Clearly not. Unresolved problems affect each employee, their teams, and their departments. They undermine employees' interest, ability to express themselves fully in their work, and attitudes—their level of stagnation deepens.

The need for a common process to identify and understand a problem, understand its components, evaluate alternative solutions, and recommend a viable, understandable solution is loud and clear. Employees need a common foundation of thought and language for understanding, communicating, collaborating, resolving, and celebrating.

Progressive thinking, learning organizations that are committed to creating an organization full of vitality view employee learning and participation in problem solving as critical for everyone, at all levels.

When employees have a common process, are given permission and encouragement to address problems, and receive recognition for their initiative and participation with new opportunities for their own future, feelings of empowerment take hold. The feeling of being stuck with no solution dissolves and enthusiasm takes root. That's Vitality!

NOTES

Actions: _____

_____

_____

_____

_____

Call Whom: _____

_____

_____

_____

_____

By When: _____

_____

_____

_____

_____

"Lack of conditions for self-realization leads to stagnation...."

– SUNDAY ADELAJA

SECTION 3
SHARED LEARNING CREATES VITALITY

*"Tell me and I forget, teach me and I may remember,
involve me and I learn."*

– BENJAMIN FRANKLIN

CHAPTER 9

CROSS-TRAINING IS SHARED LEARNING

"CROSS-TRAINING" IS A COMMON PRACTICE TODAY. IT IS A term most often used in relation to sports and fitness as "[t]he action or practice of engaging in two or more sports or types of exercise in order to improve fitness or performance in one's main sport.[25] "In other arenas, cross-training is referred to as "[t]he action or practice of training or being trained in more than one role or skill." Cross-training is well practiced in some organizations. In others, it is a familiar but is largely unpracticed.

In reality, we have practiced cross-training since childhood. We learned and shared chores as a family to help the household run. We cross-trained in school as we learned a variety of subjects to construct a career. As adults, we cross-trained and shared learning in order to care for our children. Then in business, the focus began to change.

In business, the focus became specialization—intense knowledge in a very narrow lane. Today's accelerating world requires fast response and interaction to survive. Just working with a chain of specialties is no longer viable.

To create sharper responsiveness, there is increasing focus on cross-training, or "multi-skilling." Multi-skilling involves training employees to be flexible in response to changing schedules and situations. Some employee experts think of cross-training as a "disaster recovery plan" or a way to become more valuable to the company. And in the military, cross-training is part of everyday life.

Referencing Matt McKay of Chron, many advantages exist to cross-training employees. Employees become more familiar with the business culture and operation. They can fill in for each other when someone is absent. Teamwork is easier and comradeship increases; understanding of one's job and value increases and misunderstandings are reduced.

From Cross-Training to Shared Learning

The concept of training is well known and important for all organizations. They have training budgets, training departments, training leaders, and training coaches. They have training courses, training curricula, and training schedules. Training is most often offered in a classroom with a set time and schedule on-line, with little or no on-time mentoring. Plus, training per employee is generally offered only once or twice a year, and continual training is rare.

Occasionally, training takes the form of internships, periods of time for an employee to work in another department or under the direct auspices of a particular individual. Unfortunately, the number of employees who experience these sponsored internships after their first year of employment is very low.

The rate of change in the market and in organizations is accelerating. The need for greater collaboration and responsiveness is exponential. More and more employees want and need cross-training to keep up. Can occasional training in classrooms fill this need? Can it loosen the sludge of personal stagnation? Can online training without hands-on practice and mentoring fit the bill? Can organizations keep up without evolving their workforce? Is simply replacing the entire workforce over time the answer? Or do you need a new idea—a new way to reach more employees, incent more interest, and be more prepared?

Shared Learning Is Progressive!

Shared learning builds on the belief that employee potential, regardless of how long it has been asleep, can wake up. It says employee resistance to waking up their own personal potential is just non-belief in their own capabilities, a thought often reinforced by their work environment.

Shared learning starts with the premise that we *can* and *must* Vitalize employee belief in their own potential. Effective shared learning starts with basic core skills that 1) require communication and collaboration, and 2) begin to address causes of stagnation. It starts with learning skills that are taught, recognized, and rewarded everywhere across the organization so employees can participate anytime, anywhere.

The first step is to require shared learning in critical core skills across the organization so employees know the organization is serious about freeing employee potential. It recognizes that all employees can learn more, do more, communicate more, and collaborate more, and as a result, can give more.

The next step is to develop actionable ideas for "expanded opportunity." Expanded opportunity may mean working with another employee in the trainee's area of interest. It can mean attending strategic planning and brainstorming sessions in their own and other departments. It can mean a mentoring program to recognize formally the employee's level of experience and education to date, and dialogue about what is required next to enhance the employee's confidence and potential.

The next significant step is to expand practical, experiential learning opportunities so employees can better understand the business and build confidence that enables greater participation. Such opportunities can include touring a manufacturing line, spending a day in shipping, or being introduced to the functions adjacent to their own jobs.

When this learning is supported with a system that respectfully tracks their participation and progress, and relates their increasing experience to the opening of new opportunities to learn, willing participation increases. Employees know you are paying attention—that you are not ignoring them. Stagnation decreases, Vitality increases!

In Chapter 10, we begin to introduce new programs that apply well-known skills in a new way. These new programs illustrate shared learning—the mutual learning and shared application of skills that accelerate employee ability to participate in problem solving, creating new ideas and solutions, and mentoring other employees. They are specific tangible actions that can be implemented today across your organization to begin Vitalizing your workforce.

CHAPTER 9
SUMMARY

VITALIZE YOUR WORKFORCE INCLUDES CREATING A SUSTAINable Vitalized culture that instills a new sense of freedom and opportunity for employees. It requires consistent and quality oversight of their new interaction with peers, other functions, and other departments to ensure progressive learning that allows for positive, beneficial sequences of experience that can lead to expanded job opportunities.

Shared learning asks employees to delegate and mentor other employees in what they know, helping to build a highly supportive internal culture where mentoring is the norm. Shared learning means that learning critical skills is not for just a few select employees; rather it is a requirement for everyone, in every level and every function, to create a highly responsive organization.

Shared learning means establishing a level of communication in these critical skills so employees can understand and participate wherever they are, in any situation. They may not be able to make strategic decisions, but their newly expanded awareness, confidence, and practice with the new skills increases their day-to-day value to the organization and exponentially heightens their respect for their own potential.

NOTES

Actions: _____

_____

_____

_____

_____

Call Whom: _____

_____

_____

_____

_____

By When: _____

_____

_____

_____

_____

"The inability to delegate is one of the biggest problems I see with managers at all levels."

– ELI BROAD

CHAPTER 10

DYNAMIC DELEGATION

STAGNATION IS NOT A SMALL PROBLEM! LEADERS MUST adopt quantum-leap thinking to remedy employee stagnation. Leaders must declare their commitment to becoming a progressive thinking, learning organization that has vitality and a rapid, effective way to solve problems, address emergencies, meet challenges, and reach for opportunities as they arise.

Teams that best exemplify this vitality and extraordinary collaboration today are our emergency first-responders, hospital Emergency Room teams, and military units that demonstrate tactical fluidity as described in General Stanley McChrystal's book, *Team of Teams*. Their responsibilities require rapid idea exchange, quick sharing of duties, and split-second collaboration.

Yet, in many corporations and organizations, employees are still required to sit in the same chair, day after day, year after year, with no change in their job or understanding of the organization as a whole, with mouths and minds closed. And we wonder why they are stagnant. Where have their dreams gone? How are they using their natural-born talents? Where is their self-esteem and confidence to offer and do more?

Every employee on every level, including the CEO, has something on his or her desk that won't allow for learning anything more by doing again. Performing the same work, over and over again, with no new learning or expansion of perspective is a sure recipe for stagnation.

> "Vitalizing your organization is no longer an option.
> It is an imperative."

Dynamic Delegation is a low-cost, high-reward shared-learning program that can be implemented across your organization, from the top down. Dynamic Delegation enables continual sharing of information and skill transfer from one employee to another, on a highly practical (hands-on) level with mentoring from those who know how to accomplish the task. This shared learning expands communication and collaboration; and importantly, enables employees to participate actively in both remediating their own stagnation and learning new skills, including mentoring.

Why Raise Delegation as a New Thought?

Delegation is a common term. However, in reality, how widely is it taught or applied? By whom? And where? A *Harvard Business Review* study of 322 companies found that only 28 percent of companies and organizations provided any form of delegation training.[26] Receiving more work to do is a common experience. Having the opportunity to give or delegate work to others is not.

Why is delegation training important? How can we apply it differently to overcome employee stagnation and create a new vitality?

> "Delegation has long been considered the right of the elite."

Delegation has long been considered the right of the elite—those with enough money or rank to hand off work to others. The rest of the organization generally does not have this luxury. In their own words, employees feel like "rungs on a ladder with work flowing downward, not up or out." They see no possibility of change. They are stuck and stagnant.

Today, we need to think differently.

The word *delegate* is derived directly from Latin *delagatus*, past participle of *delegare* "to send as a representative," from de—"from, away" and legare—"send with a commission."[27] There is no mention of this action being reserved only for the elite or those who can afford it. And there is no restriction on who or what can be delegated.

However, delegation alone is not enough. Mentoring is elemental to the process, i.e., providing one-on-one support while the recipient learns what the provider knows. This process is called FLOW—freedom to learn, observe, and work. When there is FLOW, no one is stagnant. FLOW means ideas and communication are in motion. FLOW is continual; it never stops.

Transforming stagnation and boredom into proactive energy does not happen overnight. It requires small repeated steps over time to expand employee perspective and increase participation. Creating a FLOW of opportunity to learn and to mentor imbues communication and teamwork skills that cannot be defined or attained any other way, across your organization and between levels.

Delegation is both a skill and an opportunity. Delegation involves:

1. Identifying task(s) to be delegated
2. Identifying another employee who will benefit the most by receiving the task
3. Knowing how to:
   - Communicate effectively the opportunity to the receiver
   - Encourage and reduce possible resistance by the receiver
   - Mentor the receiver until he or she can successfully accomplish the task independently

What Can Be Delegated?

Ask yourself, then ask your employees: Do you do anything in a day that you are not going to learn any more by doing again? You might hear laughter; then watch for a telltale sigh. You will know the answer.

In our 2014 inquiry across many industries, job descriptions, and levels, the response from 2,400 participants was universal. We heard a lot of laughter and saw many nods of agreement. Once the humor in the answer subsided, they offered their truths:

- "If someone would just move on…I could…."
- "Half of what I do, we really don't need anymore…."
- "I would have left long ago if it weren't for the benefits…."
- "Management has no idea…so they don't care…."

They were voicing stagnation, and leaders must listen. Leaders need to create a systematic way for employees to release work that is old to them so they can learn something new. The opportunity to continually learn something new lies within every organization, in every industry, at every level and function.

What percentage of your employees' jobs includes something that isn't in their job descriptions, but they do it better and faster than someone else, so they do it anyway? What percentage of their jobs do employees take on "by default" because the previous person did them? Do you know? Do your managers know? Likely not. This is stagnation hiding as "busy." Find out and start Dynamic Delegation.

Ask your employees: Do you know anyone who will learn something new and benefit by learning the parts of your job that are "old" to you? Yes! Of course you do! Everyone does, including the CEO and C-Level executives.

The real question is: Do you care? You need to care!

Vitality Is the Opposite of Stagnation

The inherent meaning of *vitality* is "vital life force." It comes from the Latin root (*italitatem, vitalitas*); from *vita* or "life," and is related to *vivere* "to live."[28]

Vitality is the creative energy of life, the creative energy that makes the grass grow and the flowers bloom. Vitality is inside everyone. It is the juice that makes us alive, happy, and interested in participating. We mean something. We can feel it. People like to feel good about themselves. They like to feel recognized, valued, and appreciated for who they are and what they do. They like to feel, while working for you, that their capacity for managing their lives and supporting their families is expanding, not diminishing.

> *"If people are bored and their potential ignored,*
> *their motivation disintegrates."*

If people are bored and their potential ignored, their motivation disintegrates. Their vital energy and interests turn in other directions. Their work becomes secondary and your business suffers. Providing a systematic way for people to delegate aspects of their work that are no longer new to them creates space and time to learn new skills and earn new opportunities.

A strong Dynamic Delegation program helps employees confidently transform their stagnant energy into more proactive communication, collaboration, and participation. A quality Dynamic Delegation program reignites interest, increases feelings of personal vitality, and opens possibilities for the future. Everyone wins: you, your employees, and your business.

Key Steps to Dynamic Delegation

1. **Require and Provide Quality Delegation Training for *All* Employees**

In the Vitality model, effective and efficient delegation is a critical skill.

"Dynamic Delegtation is not dumping!"

Quality training for delegation includes a checklist of sequential actions for both the person giving and the person receiving delegation. Issues to be addressed include:

- How to identify work to delegate
- How to select someone to receive the delegation to create a win-win for everyone
- How to communicate the delegation as a learning opportunity
- How delegation benefits the receiving person's job and career
- How to follow up with quality mentoring
- How to overcome resistance from the receiving employee
- How to share this important training with your family and your community

The Vitality of Possibility starts to emerge.

2. **Require Quality Dynamic Delegation and Mentoring Training for *All* Managers**

Dynamic Delegation training for managers is an imperative. Many managers have little or no regular communication with their own staff, hence they are not comfortable with either delegating or mentoring. These managers often claim lack of time or no personal benefit as reasons to minimize their participation in employee-improvement programs.

Further distancing themselves from their employees, traditional training *per se* has been an activity provided online or by a separate training department, often in a separate training location. The manager's only responsibility is to approve the training and enable the employee to take the time off for the training—with no follow-up required.

Organizations committed to Vitality require their managers to be pro-active people-leaders who help oversee the development of their employees' potential. If any of your managers are not proven, proactive people-leaders, then (most of) the employees under their direction are stagnant. The negative effect on your business is direct.

> "Leadership is not about attributes (personality traits), it is about behavior.... We need them (leaders) to jump into the future at an accelerated pace, no matter the size of changes required to make that happen [without Vitality across the organization].... [W]e end-up with over-managed and under-led organizations which are increasingly vulnerable in a fast-moving world."
>
> – JOHN P. KOTTER

Managers who have skills as specialists but choose to remain distant from their employees are no longer tolerable. As soon as poor people-leaders are identified, take action. Not everyone is a people-leader, and people should be respected for their choices. These managers can be offered people-leadership training with a prove-in period to demonstrate their new people motivation skills, or they can be reassigned to other departments as specialists. This change might seem small. However, reassignment of non-people-leading managers:

- Minimizes manager-created stagnation
- Signals to employees that leadership is truly listening
- Transforms employee feelings of being stuck in place, into positive feelings of opportunity for their future, one small step at a time.

Dynamic Delegation Training for managers includes:

- How to plan for Dynamic Delegation
- How to delegate both as an individual and as a manager
- How to oversee the Dynamic Delegation program within the organization
- How to work with your Corporate Vitality Team to support employee interest and career planning with planned delegation planning and tracking
- How to train natural people-leaders in the Dynamic Delegation process so they become part of your vital cross-training network
- How to measure and reward diligence in delegation and mentoring for increasing success

Communication for quality delegation and mentoring is a learned skill. The more managers and employees are trained and mentored in these valuable core skills, the more vibrant and collaborative your organization will become.

3. **Implement an Employee Delegation, Mentoring, and Tracking System**

Enlist a simple tracking system to record tasks delegated, from and to whom. This system helps assure a significant progression of learning and the building of new talent pools for new initiatives.

4. **Establish Delegation Days**

Delegation Days are pre-announced days for employees to delegate something on their desk to another employee and begin mentoring the task's recipient.

Publish an annual Delegation Day Schedule company-wide, or by location. A published schedule reinforces employee knowledge that the entire company is involved, and that leadership is committed to accelerating Corporate Vitality. The Delegation Day Schedule gives managers time to communicate with their employees about which tasks they can delegate, when, and why. Scheduled Delegation Days allow for advanced planning, assure delegation doesn't disrupt workflow, and encourage discussion about workload management as well as opportunities to learn new skills.

A Delegation Day Schedule also makes recordkeeping easier. Your Corporate Vitality Team (see Chapter 19) can lead a process to track the tasks delegated and supported with mentoring, and tracks from whom and to whom the tasks were delegated. The purpose of tracking is to ensure that everyone is included, and to ensure a continual beneficial FLOW of learning.

Employees and their supervisors will soon look forward to Delegation Days as opportunities to increase their awareness, interest, vitality, and involvement in their work and careers.

5. **Give Employees Permission Both to Delegate and Ask for More Delegation**

Two important parts of the Dynamic Delegation process are: delegating something old and learning something new.

"People with high personal initiative will become self-evident."

Instilling Vitality in a well-managed delegation and mentoring program enables everyone to progress at the rate that is best for them. Giving employees who learn quickly or have high personal initiative permission to ask for more tasks to be delegated to them with mentoring provides a sense of freedom and sparks feelings of new possibility.

Learning four new tasks in a given year may be easy for some and challenging for others. And still others will find it easy to learn four new tasks in a day. Encourage employees who demonstrate personal initiative to ask for more delegation when they are ready. Employees with high personal initiative will become self-evident regardless of formal education and job level. You likely will "see" these individuals for the first time. That's progress.

The Dynamic Delegation process enables consistent visibility for high initiative employees; enables networking among employees with common interests; and facilitates communication, collaboration, and dynamic teaming.

6. **High Pass-Along Goodwill**

Encouraging employees to share their delegation and mentoring training outside the organization—at home and in their communities—can be greatly beneficial for them and for company goodwill. It helps reinforce employees' use and practice of their new skills and instills an important sense of positive leadership. The more employees share these skills with the groups and organizations they know, the more confidence they gain and the more goodwill is generated for your company.

The AT&T Pioneer Program is an excellent example. Employees are encouraged to participate in community-building activities. This participation enhances teamwork, relationships, and respect; and employees feel good about themselves and the company. Cummins is also committed to the communities in which it works. In 2012, Cummins' Every Employee Every Community (EEEC) initiative enabled 27,000 Cummins CME employees to work on community service projects. The program's success is attributed to the strengthening of employee relationships in an enjoyable social dimension to work where colleagues feel connected and productivity improves.[29]

CHAPTER 10
SUMMARY

DYNAMIC DELEGATION IS A NEW CONCEPT. THE WORLD IS moving too fast to tolerate stagnation of employee potential on any level, or in any function.

> *"...over-managed and under-led organizations are increasingly vulnerable in a fast-moving world."*
>
> – JOHN P. KOTTER

Leaders must adopt quantum-leap thinking to remedy employee stagnation. They must commit to creating a progressive thinking, learning organization that hones creating a new competitive edge by developing employee potential across the workforce.

Dynamic Delegation declares that occasional budget-limited training, a few times a year, to a few employees is not going to solve the problem. Stagnation is the result of daily long-term control of employee time, interests, and opportunities to the deference of a few. Stagnation results from crushed initiative. New learning must be continual and experienced by all employees to create a common language base and understanding of the activity. With management support, an organization can change employee beliefs from "no opportunity" to a belief in "continual opportunity."

The Vitalize Dynamic Delegation Program embraces all employees, creating a shared responsibility for the awakening, evolution, and new application of employee talents, skills, and interests. It requires the systematic forwarding of tasks that are "old" to one employee (they won't learn anything more by doing it again), and offering the task to someone who will benefit by learning something new.

Requiring the learning and practice of quality delegation and mentoring across the organization creates FLOW—freedom to learn, observe, and work. Feelings of being stuck diminish; learning a progression of new skills for new opportunities becomes easier. Levels of confidence, interest, and loyalty rise. That is Vitality!

NOTES

Actions: _____

_____

_____

_____

_____

Call Whom: _____

_____

_____

_____

_____

By When: _____

_____

_____

_____

_____

> "A mentor is someone who allows you to see the hope inside yourself."
>
> – OPRAH WINFREY

CHAPTER 11

ESTABLISHING UNIVERSAL MENTORING

MENTORING IS ONE OF THE MOST POWERFUL, ENGAGING, lasting interactions we humans can engage in, and we are entering an era when mentoring in all directions is more important than ever—up, down, sideways, and sometimes in circles, as teams accelerate training and mentoring each other.

What Is Mentoring?

Webster's Dictionary defines a mentor as "a trusted counselor or guide." Mentoring is a long-term relationship in which or through which someone gradually imparts wisdom, guidance, and support to another who wants to learn. A mentor is not a counselor or a coach. Nor does a mentor oversee or become part of day-to-day activities. A mentor is a personal advocate for someone's life who takes a respectful, caring long-range view of a mentee's growth and development.

The mentoring relationship is private, where the building of significant two-way trust enables the exploration of questions, learning, fears, and expansion of perspectives. Mentors share ideas, explore risks, evaluate alternatives, create high-level action plans, recognize successes, and review efforts.

A mentor has no ulterior motive—no service or product to sell. Mentors can share important lessons from their experience to help the mentee learn more quickly. They can introduce people who can increase understanding in areas of interest, and help expand the mentee's personal business network.

Who Needs Mentoring?

Mentoring is important for everyone—people of all ages and in all situations of life. We all need mentoring to expand our talents and experience more of who we are. We all need support to gain confidence in learning something new, enlarge our perspectives, and hone our skills. Young children need mentoring to learn about the world around them and to gain confidence in learning important skills, such as math and reading. Young people need mentors to teach them sports or hobbies they are interested in so they can succeed safely with the greatest amount of enjoyment.

The benefits of mentoring are clearly measurable. Young adults who receive mentoring get better grades in school and are 52 percent less likely to skip a day of school.[30] Mentored students are 55 percent more likely to enroll in college and 78 percent more likely to volunteer. Ninety percent are interested in becoming mentors themselves, and 93 percent are more likely to hold leadership positions.[31]

This need for mentoring continues throughout our lives. Today, the need for mentoring in business is greater than ever before. New entrants in the workforce require mentoring to broaden their organizational perspective as quickly as possible. Boomers want mentoring to redirect their expertise as the needs of the business change. Employees who have little experience working in technical environments need mentoring to learn new skills and how to work successfully with accelerated schedules. Executives need mentoring to learn how to lead increasingly complex workforces in an unrelenting, increasingly chaotic world. Everyone needs mentoring. We can't do it alone.

Yet, as questioned by Meghan Biro, a *Forbes* magazine contributor, "where have all the business mentors gone?" There are far less business mentors than before, and that is taking a dramatic toll on companies. After rapid expansion at Toyota, there were not enough senior managers able to take junior managers under their wing, and many of the new managers did not know the culture or how to get things accomplished. New employees coming from universities knew their areas of study but not how be employees, how to work to a schedule, how to create and work as a team, or how to communicate effectively.

We are facing the same challenges. It is our responsibility now to understand this burgeoning need for mentoring, not as a trial but as an opportunity to vitalize our workforce. We must change the paradigm of how we think about our employees, how we share information, and how we infuse employee potential with new opportunity and wisdom. We need to devise new ways to mentor all employees across the organization so that spontaneous communication and collaboration becomes as natural as breathing.

Gens X, Y, and Z are Defining the Way

The expanding "what's in it for me" demands of Gens X, Y, and Z are helping show us the way. These generations are coming into the workforce with vast experience in social media and other technologies that they have used throughout their schooling to search for and find information instantaneously. They are bold in asking friends and calling people they don't know for leads to learning more and becoming more. They are bringing this unmasked "ask immediately, don't wait" attitude and behavior with them into corporate environments that are often cumbersome and designed for controlled systematic growth.

In a 2016 Deloitte Millennial Survey, Millennials (Generation Y) were asked how they felt about having a mentor. An astonishing 94 percent of Millennial employees felt mentors provided good advice about the organization and their jobs, and many preferred the calm wisdom and insights provided by Boomers. Mentoring is particularly important for retaining new Millennial employees. Of the 68 percent of Millennial employees who received mentoring, all said they planned to stay with their organization for at least five years, as compared to 34 percent who did not. When considering the 100-300 percent annual salary cost to replace an employee, the direct financial value of mentoring is clearly significant.

Millennials are also a "feedback-loving" generation. The more feedback they receive, the more they want "stretch goals," goals that make them reach for more. They desire to test themselves and their skills. The immediate benefit is that the more stretch goals are desired by your employees, the more work you can assign. This is great—*if* your culture and your managers are prepared to be people-leaders and provide challenge goals, feedback, and opportunities. That's power leadership. If they are not, your target results may be only a dream.

CEOs are people too. Mentors are imperative. CEOs are making more and more critical decisions every day, and at a faster rate. As shared by Meghan Biro, they are often breaking new ground and continually seek information from advisors who can counsel them on their work or problems. In a *Harvard Business Review* study of forty-five CEOs with formal mentoring arrangements, 71 percent were certain that company performance had improved as a result.[32]

A Dangerous Predicament

How about the rest of the organization? According to Dobbs and Madgavkar, by the year 2020, there will be a possible shortage of work among 13 percent of highly skilled, college-educated employees, equaling around 38- to 40-million workers. How did we arrive in this dangerous predicament? What is the problem? Too specialized perhaps?

Originally people handed down a new skill through one-on-one mentoring in a trade. With the Industrial Age came a hierarchical system that included managers, supervisors, and training departments. One-on-one mentoring faded as an important skill for most employees and became a specialty perk for the few employees selected for top positions.

Over time, experience proved that those employees with mentoring achieved more than those without. Mentoring became an employee advantage, managed through the Human Resources Department. With the advent of diversity, this application of mentoring took yet another turn. It became a tool to help raise the value of women and minority groups. So, let's ask again, how about the rest of the organization?

To support this broader audience, talent development and corporate skill training stepped into the mix, expanding general training content and schedules. This broadened training successfully established a new baseline of skills for mid-range managers, but this approach is a) budget dependent; b) a bane for supervisors since it requires planned absenteeism from the job; and c) not applied fully or equally across many organizations. The introduction of extensive elearning programs partially solved this problem, but hands-on mentoring and practice of a skill or function is still critically absent.

The advent of "lack of employee engagement" concern and solutions to help make employees "happy" did bring some beneficial programs, such as childcare in or near work, greater scheduling flexibility, and the ability to work from home without retribution. However, many employees by now worked farther way from each other and mentoring to prepare employees new opportunities became even fuzzier or nonexistent.

So where does that leave us now? It leaves us in an accelerating world environment with technological applications that override the need for human wisdom. This situation coupled with accelerating attrition of Boomer employees who may not know the new technologies but *do* know your company, products, and customers, and an unavoidable flood of new employees who don't even know how to be employees, let alone be high contributors to your business, creates extraordinary challenges for leaders.

Are you comfortable with this? No? I can't blame you. Now what?

> "The truth is: "Most organizations
> place little emphasis on mentoring."

Does your organization view mentoring as a perk? A sideline? A critical skill? More specifically, is mentoring even in the equation? Do your executives know what mentoring is, let alone view it as relevant and important at all levels of the organization?

Of the 2,400 participants in our live inquiries, 98 percent cited that while they believed in mentoring, mentoring in their organization was still only for the "special few" management employees deemed to be worthwhile candidates. Plus, the accelerating needs and demands placed on managers left little time or attention for mentoring even a few employees.

If managers who do mentor experience an 88 percent increase in employee productivity compared with 24 percent when people only receive classroom training (Mentorcloud.com,) why is there still low emphasis on mentoring? Where is the disconnect?

> "Are we asking the wrong question—again?
> What do we need now—today?"

Let's Go Back to the Basics

When you learned to walk and talk, you observed and learned largely by trial and error. Your caregivers mentored you. You had full freedom to learn, observe, and practice.

You may have grown up in a supportive environment where asking questions to learn new skills was encouraged, respected, and celebrated.

Then you went to work. For a while, your new environment provided learning. You got the lay of the land and became familiar with the people, roles, and tools. Then what? The people who welcomed you soon disappeared into the background. Routine took over. Their initial interest in your potential and your talents faded. Perhaps your curiosity led you to visit other departments to continue learning, only to be criticized for wasting time. Perhaps you heard the repeated suggestion, "Be happy just to have a job." Your view of your potential started to fade until it became stagnant. Your hopes for your future became cloudy and maybe disappeared altogether, and you began to say, "Now what?" With this large, ignored dampening of initiative, your workforce spirals downward. First, they become resigned, then apathetic, then resentful, and finally rebellious.

Will a workforce harboring these feelings meet your company's goals? Can these employees transform your company into an organization with the Vitality to meet emerging market demands? No, they cannot. And outsourcing those positions will only produce the same or worse result—at great cost to the effectiveness of your organization *and* your bottom line.

"Replacing stagnant employees with new talent without changing the paradigm of leading them will only produce the same result."

Where Is the Vitality You Seek?

Vitality is inside each and every employee. Remember your life as a five-year-old? Take just a moment. Close your eyes. You can feel it. How wide open did you feel? The world was yours. You could be and do anything you wanted. You had dreams. You had confidence that you could be in the world and that the world would help you become all you could be. What did you want for your life?

At five years old, you were excited about everything—your red bike, an action figure, jumping in puddles, or jumping on the couch...taking a walk, playing ball, running with your dog, playing fashion designer, building a tree house, eating an ice cream cone, or laughing for no reason.

This is the vitality of life. It's elemental to people everywhere. Everyone needs to learn and experience something new, to discover more of who they are and the essence of their lives. Progressive thinking businesses know this and leverage it.

*"It is time to institute a new way of thinking.
It is time to change the inside game."*

It is time to ask, "What is the true reward that humans need to increase their interest and participation?" Millennials ask the question:

"What is in it for me?" You can provide the answer by providing a clearer path to what's in it for them.

Money and promotion are no longer key drivers. Are they necessary? Yes, but employees now see them as occasional handouts that might or might not be awarded. Does that stimulate personal motivation? No!

Expanding individual potential

Expanding individual potential and opportunity is the primary driver. Your dreams for your company's future and your employees' dreams are not that different. They simply have a different perspective.

> "How do you vitalize your workforce
> to sharpen your competitive edge?"

Create a culture of continual problem solving and quality mentoring at all levels of your organization. Require all employees to become skilled at mentoring in order to Vitalize employee potential for all of your employees, not just a few. Encourage them to apply their problem-solving and mentoring skills outside your organization—in their homes and communities—and create recognition programs that reward them for their initiative. This is creating Vitality.

Make each day a learning opportunity. Establish programs that continue to expand employees' perspectives about their jobs and the business as a whole. Increase cross-functional or departmental interface, communication, and collaboration. Establish a Corporate Vitality Office that oversees the development of shared learning programs such as high-quality delegation and mentoring. Ensure that managers at all level that have exceptional people-leadership skills. Charge the Corporate Vitality Team with responsibility to ensure progressive learning for all employees so they can *earn* new, expanded, mentored opportunities as their clear "What's in it for me?"

> "Mentoring must be a required skill
> at every level of an organization."

To mentor someone means to guide and advise him. Mentoring is a learned skill that requires teaching, coaching, practice, repetition, and reward. This doesn't happen overnight.

You might be asking "How can we provide ongoing learning opportunities for all of our employees? We don't have a training organization or budget set up for that, nor do we want one that big, and our managers have their hands full." That is default thinking, not solutions thinking. Solutions thinking has Vitality. It radiates the "power of possibility."

Perhaps you do have solutions thinking and are asking, "How do we mentor and provide hands-on practice on such a large scale?"

These are real questions that need very real answers. Whether you have 20, 2,000, or 20,000 employees, the answer is within your organization right now. Look at your Vision and Mission. What do they actually say to your organization? Are they standard boilerplate that are written for investors and senior management and are essentially disconnected from your employees? Are you addressing the need to Vitalize your employee potential by stating your commitment to becoming a progressive thinking learning organization and what that means for your employees? Clearly define what it means to become a progressive thinking, learning organization as a goal for your corporate culture. Communicate these goals effectively to all levels and functions, and visibly confirm your intention by establishing formal problem-solving, delegation, and mentoring training programs.

Require all employees to develop quality, proactive problem-solving, delegation, and mentoring skills. Add these skill requirements to your corporate policies, hiring documents, and promotion criteria. Change the paradigm and you change the game! Your clear commitment from the top is mandatory. Establish your sincerity and give stagnant employees something they can believe in.

"Opportunity is the juice that feeds employee motivation."

Establishing a Corporate Vitality Officer function that is separate from the Human Resources function further communicates to your employees that this is a new day.

Set and Communicate Vitality Leadership Goals

Clearly communicate that it is not only time to think in a new way, but to act in a new way. Let Human Resources continue to manage hiring and firing and policies regarding government requirements and insurance. Create a separate and clear focus and accountability for the Chief Vitality Officer function to create, monitor, measure, and recognize organization-wide programs designed to dissolve stagnation, instill Vitality, and hone a new critical competitive edge for the entire organization.

CHAPTER 11
SUMMARY

MENTORING IS THE ART OF ONE PERSON FACILITATING THE learning and personal growth of another. In years gone by, people with skills and knowledge intuitively and automatically provided mentoring to pass on what they knew to people following them in that responsibility. As our culture advanced, organizations became larger, technology accelerated and became more intimate, and generic training became pervasive. Mentoring went from being the norm a hundred years ago to being a very scarce activity today.

Leaders cannot afford remote and abstract leadership now.

A critical component to Vitalizing Your Workforce is once again to create a culture that values, recognizes, and rewards mentoring as a core skill for all employees. Stimulating and encouraging people at all levels to delegate and mentor inherently increases better communication and collaboration among employees. It increases inquiry, care, and teamwork. It facilitates deepening of employee understanding of the business, one step at a time; it enhances willingness to join in problem solving and develop new ideas. In short, mentoring is a mandatory core skill for Vitalizing your organization anywhere, any time.

NOTES

Actions: _____

_____

_____

_____

_____

Call Whom: _____

_____

_____

_____

_____

By When: _____

_____

_____

_____

_____

"We are continually faced by great opportunities brilliantly disguised as insoluble problems"

– LEE IACOCCA

SECTION 4
WHAT'S IN IT FOR ME?

*"Brains, like hearts,
go where they are appreciated."*

– ROBERT MCNAMARA

CHAPTER 12

ACTIVATING APPRECIATION

APPRECIATION TOUCHES THE HEART. IT RECOGNIZES someone's time, effort, and intention as worthwhile. When expressed sincerely, appreciation naturally expands the recipient's willingness to do more. Appreciation is truly food for the soul.

According to *Webster's Dictionary*, "to appreciate" means "to recognize the full worth of or to be grateful for something." The word "appreciate" is generally used in three ways:

1. When asking someone to do something:
"I would appreciate it if you would…."
2. As an expression when a valuable action is finished:
"Thank you. I appreciate that."
3. Or to express the value appreciation of an item,
such as a house, jewelry, or investment.

Why Is Appreciation Necessary?

We all need uplift in our lives. Negativity surrounds us via the media, movies, games, and life challenges at work and at home. Our commercial culture says we aren't good enough, and the media focuses on what is wrong in the world. We even get negative feedback from parking meters (out of time), credit cards (payment due), credit scores (late payment), and banks ($$ spent). Do any of them say, "Good job for all the times you do something right?"

At work, how many times a day, week, or month does someone recognize you or your work? Your ideas? Has anyone said, "I appreciate you" lately? It is common to ask someone to do more: "I would appreciate it if…" without any thought of giving something in return. And it is even more common to say, "Thank you. I appreciate that!" almost as a default habit, again without any thought of balance—or giving back.

Without appreciation, employees feel more and more frustrated, isolated, and worn out, with no solution in sight. Feelings of being overlooked, taken for granted, and even forgotten continually weaken employee willingness to participate and give more. These feelings might not be obvious, but they create a stagnation of spirit and a resignation that caring will get them nowhere.

Having a common logo on paychecks, clothing, mugs, and email might be nice. It creates a visual sense of community and belonging. But under the surface, without recognition and appreciation, there is little or no substance. Employees increasingly feel alone and stuck.

> *"We all need uplift in our lives."*

Performance Appraisals

Performance appraisals are a scheduled administrative practice with a specific process and intention. They systematically document achievements, can clarify strengths and weaknesses, and can help compare effort and results among employees. They provide a structured way to allocate raises, and they can highlight exceptional employees for advancement.

Often, however, employees work for managers who have little or no people-leadership skills and no interest in employee recognition, skill enhancement, or motivation. These managers have little interface with their employees and conduct their appraisals as a perfunctory exercise, rather than from firsthand knowledge of the employee or his or her actual job performance. Couple this with low funding for raises and low opportunity for job improvement, and you have employees who are increasingly stagnant—without personal recognition, appreciation, or opportunity. They are stuck.

Employees who work in these situations feel like numbers on a list, nothing more. Over time, the employees' contribution is the same, nothing more. They are locked into stagnation, their interest and productivity in decline. Are these employees interested in following your lead to a new direction? Not likely.

Human Resources Files (HR Files)

Most employees know that their company maintains employee records of hire date, salary, benefits, appraisals, and more. Many companies have a Human Resources department or expert to oversee these employee records. These files are private in order to protect personal employee information and enable silent management of salaries, benefits, performance appraisals, and more. The personal nature of these files makes privacy imperative. Kept under lock and key, they are not generally available, and rightly so.

However, for many employees, HR files have an ominous quality to them. Every appraisal—good or bad—goes into the file. Managers can add a rightful or wrongful complaint or evaluation, thereby influencing raises, promotions, and other opportunities—deserved or not. Employees can't change it, can't challenge it, and often can't even see it. This gives the HR file a negative connotation.

At the moment, there is no visible, tangible, or practical counterbalance to the perceived negativity of this file for employees.

What Is the Underlying Problem?

There is no process to record day-to-day employee value, demonstrated talent, attitude or participation in a way that employees can hear or see. This is not a "social work" issue. It is a human need. It is important to recognize both small and large employee contributions, whether job-related or just voluntary actions that lighten the day.

Managers who are not people-leaders make the situation worse. Their focus is usually on their own job and their own promotion, with little real thought or communication with their staff. This self-focus and lack of recognition deflates motivation. Frustration, increased negativity, and decreasing loyalty create organizational strife.

Five Reasons Leaders Do Not Address the Appreciation Problem:

1. The problem is not big enough to worry about (yet).
2. Our employees aren't children. Adults don't need handholding.

3. Solutions are expensive.
4. Solutions will take time away from my other duties.
5. I don't care.

The solutions are relatively simple, but they won't create themselves! Give managers the right tools, with the right incentives, and they will use them. The right tools will require managers to communicate with their employees regularly through actions that consistently benefit the employees.

Conversely, if you don't give managers easy-to-use tools to support employee recognition and appreciation, by default, managers become part of the problem. They become an added reason for employee frustration, and managers, too, become increasingly stagnant.

Simple recognition and appreciation tools can increase interest and feelings of wellbeing and worthiness that deepen commitment to go the extra mile.

Is "Thank You" obsolete?

Thank You is not obsolete. It is obscure.

The rapid pace of life today stems largely from accelerating technologies in commerce, communication, video games, and more. Taking time to care almost seems a luxury. Our now pervasive 3.5-second attention span among employees and management alike makes a sincere *Thank You* a rarity and often an ingenuous habitual statement, with hardly a glance at the receiver. Sad, but true.

Even in good work relationships, the value of a heartfelt *Thank You* earned over time can disappear in a second. Consider a good working relationship between a manager and employee, where respect and trust is strong. When the manager gets promoted, moves to another department, or leaves the company, what happens to the employee who received the *Thank You*? That deserving employee is left high and dry to begin again with the new manager.

Some readers might say, "That's okay. Good employees just do their work." Careful! This is business-as-usual thinking. That cycle has run out!

"Can you lead employees who don't want to be there?"

Today, market research data confirms that 65 percent of employees who are not recognized are looking for another job.[33] "What's in it for me?" quickly turns into "Why should I work here?"

And they are serious!

Can you lead employees who don't want to be there? Can you ask employees who are planning to leave to work harder? Can you afford to replace 65 percent of your workforce? What is the cost of replacing so many employees? And how often? Where is your corporate vitality? Where is your internal competitive edge?

Where Is the Balance Between Affordable and Effective Appreciation?

Where is the balance? How do you provide the humanness to help people feel appreciated and cared for—part of something great? How can leaders connect with employees so employees want to invest more time and effort to achieve new goals?

The answer: Establish a company-wide Appreciation File Program that applies to both managers and employees, supported fully by Human Resources Administrators. The Appreciation File Program is risk-free, cost-effective, and easily implemented across any organization.

What are Appreciation Files? They are files personalized with the employee's name and the current calendar year that are located near and managed by the manager. Unlike the HR File, the Appreciation File belongs to the employee. It is a file used to retain positive feedback from anywhere in the organization at any time. The feedback can be recognition in some tangible form—a written note, a card, a reference. It may include recognition for working extra hours, exceptional effort, ideas that made a difference, thoughtful suggestions, finding solutions, and teamwork. The file provides a lasting emotional and career reference for a job well done. If a manager departs, the employee now has a tangible file that supports his or her effort and life going forward.

The employee can see and have the file any time to support pursuit of new opportunities, interviews inside the company or outside the organization, application for volunteer work, or provide for family show-and-tell. Instituting this program universally encourages awareness and underscores the importance of providing tangible appreciation, increasing the organization's Vitality.

The Appreciation File Program is sustainable and easy to implement:

1. Add this Employee Vitality Program to your new Corporate Culture as new evidence of thinking a different way.
2. Add the Appreciation File to your Corporate Policy Statements as required people-leadership tools for all managers.
3. Require active use of the Appreciation Files as proof of manager people-leadership, encouraging greater communication, collaboration, and appreciation among their employees.
4. Personalize an Appreciation File for each employee every year. Requiring a new Appreciation File each year assures the file and the process will not get lost at the back of the manager's desk, out of sight, out of mind. It also lets employees know there is ongoing interest in them as individuals and in their careers.
5. Require managers to plan time with their staff to review the contents of the employee's Appreciation File with the employee at the end of the year; physically provide the File to the employee, and provide a new file for the new year. This process represents continued awareness and encouragement by the manager to Vitalize their workforce.

NOTE: This file is not in conflict with the normal appraisal process or HR File. The Appreciation File focuses on supporting employee life-value and self-esteem with collected examples of character and contribution that is available for the employee any time.

Benefits of Personalization

Having an Appreciation File assures employees that someone is paying attention and cares about who they are and the good things they do. The employee is no longer just a number. This simple action is significant incentive for employees to continue expanding their contributions to the organization, especially since ultimately this file belongs to and benefits them.

Immediate and Long-Term Benefits

The Appreciation File facilitates increased communication between the manager and the employee. The program places attention on the employee's future, whether inside or outside the organization.

- The employee can see his or her Appreciation File expanding.
- The employee is not left hanging in limbo when a manager or mentor moves on. When a new manager arrives, he or she accepts the responsibility for continuing the Appreciation File Program.
- The Appreciation File belongs to the employee. It resides in the manager's office for safekeeping and is available for the employee to review or use any time.

The Appreciation File supports employee rewards and recognition, expanded work opportunities, and advancement within the organization. It can also contribute to applications for jobs outside the company, without ramification.

Managers who are not people-leaders and do not participate in this program will become self-evident to HR as an example of poor people-leadership, and may add rationale for reassignment to a non-people leader position.

The Appreciation File Program is a low-cost, no-risk action confirming the organization's commitment to being a progressive thinking, Vitalized workplace that values its employees.

CHAPTER 12
SUMMARY

APPRECIATION TOUCHES THE HEART. IT RECOGNIZES SOMEone's time, effort, and intention as worthwhile. When expressed sincerely, appreciation naturally expands the recipient's willingness to do more. When feeling overlooked, taken for granted, and even forgotten, employees become reluctant and resistant. This causes employee stagnation.

Performance appraisals are often a perfunctory exercise administered by a detached manager, rather than an actual report based on firsthand knowledge of the employee's value. When coupled with low salary increases and few opportunities for promotion, employees get stuck, and you enter into a stalemate. Low interest equals poor productivity.

HR files often have a negative connotation since they have no positive counterbalance. Simple recognition and appreciation tools increase employee feelings of wellbeing and worthiness. Market research confirms that 65 percent of employees who are not recognized are looking for another job. The prevailing attitude of "What's in it for me?" quickly turns into "Why should I work here?"

Where is the balance? Establish a company-wide Appreciation File Program for both managers and employees. The Appreciation File can support employee rewards and recognition as well as assignment to opportunities for expanded work experience. Appreciation Files are a no-risk, cost-effective, visible way to demonstrate your company's dedication to Vitalizing Your Workforce.

NOTES

Actions: _____

_____

_____

_____

_____

Call Whom: _____

_____

_____

_____

_____

By When: _____

_____

_____

_____

_____

"People work for money but go the extra mile for recognition, praise and rewards."

– DALE CARNEGIE

CHAPTER 13

RECOGNITION AND CELEBRATION— MAKE THEM REAL

"Can't afford it...."

"Not in the budget...."

"We aren't allowed to celebrate...."

I WISH I COULD SAY THESE AREN'T REAL STATEMENTS FROM real managers reflecting the attitudes from their leadership, but they are real. Out of the 2,400 participants in our inquiry, less than 10 percent indicated their company offered a proactive recognition program. Celebration was rare.

Delving deeper, we asked, what kind of recognition *did* they see? Most often the answer was, "We are just expected to do our job and not anticipate much, if anything. It is just the way they (management) are."

To date, the standard reward target for most employees has been the idea of a raise, bonus, or promotion. Unfortunately, over time the value of these rewards has diminished in reality. Their application often appears arbitrary, certainly not dependable, and often have little relationship to the amount of effort expended.

The Maryland Teachers Union is a good example. Its members worked hard to become a national example of excellence in education, effectively changing their teaching requirements and processes to meet government mandates year after year. Their reward: zero pay raise for years, with little or no personal recognition. How exhausting and denigrating for employees who wanted to enjoy their jobs and wanted to respect their employers too.

"A one-way win does not work."

Is this recognition? Certainly not the kind required to inspire a progressive thinking, learning organization that has Vitality with optimistic energetic employees! And certainly not the kind of recognition required to keep and motivate employees who want to enjoy working for your company.

We all come into the world with the need for recognition. Recognition for who we are as individuals and for what we can do. When we were young, caregivers around us encouraged us to smile, talk, walk, learn, and play…together. The attention gave us the belief that we were unique, that we were special and capable. We celebrated birthdays and graduations. We celebrated sports achievements, weddings, and newborn children. Life was full of recognition and celebration.

Then we come to work and what happened?

We spend at least one-third of our lives working and what do we celebrate? Very little, if anything at all. We may celebrate Wednesday because the week is half over, or Friday because the week is over. Employees celebrate each other's current life events, maybe talk about a birthday, a new car, or a new house. But what about honoring the employees themselves? What happened to celebrating them being "special" and "capable"? Are employees out of sight, out of mind? Perhaps.

A relationship is a two-way street. Without recognition, relationships disintegrate over time.

Maslow Is Still Right—
Pay Attention!

Abraham Maslow, an American psychologist, is best known for creating Maslow's Hierarchy of Needs: a theory of psychological health based on ranking innate human needs.[34] At the top of the list is self-actualization. Maslow understood that on the elemental level of basic human needs, we are all the same.

Maslow's Hierarchy of Needs

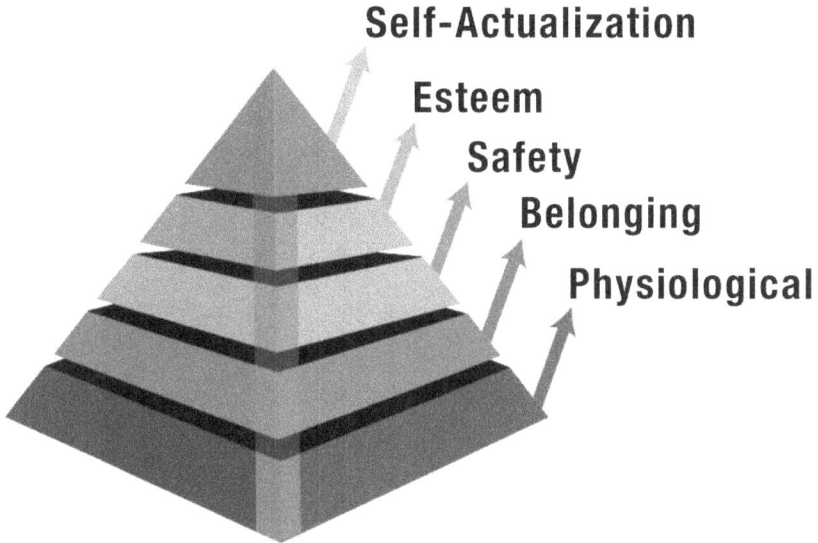

We all strive for self-actualization—all of us. As part of creation, we all need to emerge. We all have a need to reach up. We need to grow taller and stronger inside. We want to enjoy more of who we are, and what we have to give.

Work provides a roof, food, and a good measure of physical safety. With those ends in mind, we come to work, do our job, and go home. Wearing the same logo and working on a project or team together helps create an important sense of belonging. But what happens when no one makes an effort to recognize or celebrate individuals, their team, or their work? Over time, these employees become as remote as your thoughts about them. They become aware that although they work for a paycheck, they want to work for more. They want to experience more of who they really are—in this lifetime.

The more they feel ignored and unrecognized, the more their internal self-esteem disintegrates. They know they can do more and be more, but their desire for self-actualization suffocates.

The painful effects of individual stagnation are real and measurable:

- healthcare costs increase due to depression, anger, and frustration
- negativity and complaining create conflicts and disruption

- employees leave early and come in late because they don't want to be there
- loyalty declines
- finally, they leave you

Sound familiar? You can transform these situations easily and effectively by applying the principles of Vitalize Your Workforce.

Change Your Focus

"Effective recognition and celebration can be low-cost and highly successful!"

When creating recognition programs, avoid common actions and communications that don't work, such as:

- "Blanket" rewards: praising a whole department when a specific group actually did the work
- Cash rewards: money vanishes quickly and so does the memory of the money so it has no lasting value
- Ambiguity: an unclear reason or selection for the reward has a lasting negative impact

These rewards are over-used, have little or no personal recognition, and are easily forgotten.

What does work?

- Enlist input from the team about what reward they would prefer, or what their team leader would like to receive if they succeed.
- Make the recognition visible with a lasting effect.
- Focus on the recipient's accomplishment. Educate while you celebrate. Help the audience learn what the employee did to gain the recognition so the audience can gain recognition too.
- Encourage continual recognition. Share the recognition with the employee's family, the community, and with your suppliers. Sharing recognition encourages interest and inquiry, enabling the employee to talk about his or her achievement and experience the benefits. This is lasting reward.

RECOGNITION AND CELEBRATION—MAKE THEM REAL

"Customers and suppliers like to work with companies that celebrate their people!"

Change your focus. Opportunities abound for promoting your employees. Instead of small token rewards, consider highlighting the work of an employee so his or her work becomes a model for others. Some of the easiest are:

- Write an article for your newsletter with a photo. Frame copies of the article and place one in the hallway, one in the employee's office, and importantly, send one home to his or her family.

- What is the value? The employee feels honored for his contribution, and he becomes a model for others. Employees in other departments will notice and add their own applause. Suppliers and customers will express congratulations. Families will learn more about the employee and, more often than not, place the framed article somewhere visible for friends and family to see.

- Write a press release and send it with a photo to the local newspaper, frame a copy as above, place a copy in their Appreciation File, and send one home.

- Create a podcast interview with the recipient and place it on your intranet. If you can, include or mention everyone involved—suppliers, customers, and organizations—and send them the podcast link. This is cross-promotion that all organizations love. Now you are a company that not only celebrates your own people, but your associates as well. They may post the podcast on *their* intranet!

- Share the recognition with your employee groups as an opportunity for more inspiration, education, and team building.

- Create a surprise recognition with the help of the employee's team. One group bought a vanity license plate with "#1 Champ" printed on it and attached it to the back of his car without telling him. He didn't know it until someone passing by said, "Hey, congratulations on being the #1 Champ!" He had to get out of the car and walk around to the back of the car to see what the person was talking about. He was touched by his team's care. Five years later, the plate is still there, and people still ask about his work!

Adjust What You Currently Think Is of Value to Your Employees

The default choices for recognition and celebration are usually money or paid time off. These may not be the most important rewards for some of your employees, and their use may actually limit a reward of higher intrinsic value.

"Life value is real value."

What if you canvassed your employees and generated a list of twenty different ways they would like to be recognized and celebrated for their contributions? What if the list included childcare or eldercare, music lessons, or maybe a membership at a local gym? What if you identified five to seven meaningful ways to recognize and support your employees at their particular time of life, right now?

Would they appreciate working for your company? Would they leave you to work for the company down the street that has no recognition programs like yours? Would you gain marketable goodwill?

Once you identify the most highly desired ways to provide recognition, the reward becomes a two-way benefit—relieving employee tension while reducing healthcare costs for you. [It is important to note that significant accounting advantages may exist for provision of employee support programs rather than a raise or bonus cash outlay.]

Consider an on-site internship in an area of interest to your employee as a reward. A significant number of employees are placed in jobs due to company need, jobs that do not align with their interest, natural talent, or choice. Internships in a work area of their choice may be more than enough to Vitalize stagnant employees. Light the fire of possibility and you will easily gain more hours, more commitment, more communication, and more loyalty than ever before.

Providing need-specific rewards creates a high public relations opportunity for your company. Start a PR campaign exemplifying your leadership in Vitalizing your workforce. Add employee Vitality communiqués to your intranet with links to your customers, affiliates, and suppliers. Attract top talent by highlighting attainments by managers exemplifying Vitality behaviors—what you are looking for.

- Humanize everything you do. Life value is real value.
- Think out of the box.

- Think leadership that earns employee loyalty and care.
- Think leadership as a progressive thinking, learning organization that Vitalizes its employees as the new critical competitive edge.

CHAPTER 13
SUMMARY

OUT OF THE 2,400 PARTICIPANTS IN OUR INQUIRY, LESS THAN 10 percent indicated their company had a proactive recognition program for employees. Celebration for almost anything was rare. A relationship is a two-way street. Without recognition, relationships disintegrate over time. It is a choice.

Strong recognition and celebration doesn't have to be expensive—just effective! Here are some effective suggestions:

- Ask each team and team leader what they would like as a reward.
- Create recognition that has a visible, lasting effect.
- Exemplify the situation, actions, and results you are rewarding so other employees learn how they can gain recognition as well.
- Create awareness of the recognition with peers, suppliers, affiliates, and their families. All will help make the recognition lasting.
- Create opportunities for applause outside the organization that encourage others to inquire and dialogue about the employee's achievement.

Humanize everything you do. Meaningful recognition and celebration increases loyalty and vitality. Life value is real value. Think out of the box. Think of leadership in terms of being a progressive thinking, learning organization that Vitalizes employees as the new critical competitive edge.

NOTES

Actions: _____

_____

_____

_____

_____

Call Whom: _____

_____

_____

_____

_____

By When: _____

_____

_____

_____

_____

*"Stagnation floods the mind
with thoughts of failure and slowly drowns
the will to succeed; always move forward."*

– NOEL DEJESUS

CHAPTER 14

CREATING CONTINUAL OPPORTUNITY

ONE OF THE MOST DEBILITATING, STAGNATION-CREATING situations for an employee is being in a job or situation that the employee knows will never change.

In previous chapters, we have mentioned, explored, and challenged many ways in which employee stagnation becomes embedded. We held a magnifying glass to situations that required problem solving to release stuck, negative energy and create new vibrant interaction. We introduced a new perspective on practical, achievable solutions that release stagnation at its most basic level.

We now need to look forward. How do you create a sense of future for all employees so they see a true, expanding advantage for themselves while working for you? Does occasional, undependable, low monetary reward create a sense of future? Does the lure of possible promotion create a sense of future for most employees? No. It does not. So, what will?

As humans at work, we need three things. We need an opening—a ray of light that we can see—that touches our sense that we can do more and be more. We need encouragement. Permission to accept that we *can* do more, to experiment with reaching for more. And after years of our own potential being stagnant, we need encouragement and support to learn how to reach, how to think about becoming more and contributing more.

This permission and support must be continual, not just once or twice a year. Previously, permission was considered a one-way street. Employees waited for permission from you—their management—even to think about reaching.

Today, the new definition is mutual permission. Employees need permission from you to reach. They also need to know that if they give themselves permission to reach, you will recognize and support their effort. They want to know that their reaching will be worthwhile and recognized.

Luckily, there is no definition to "reaching will be worthwhile" yet. That action is available for you to define and customize for your organization. The good thing is the definition can include clarity that continual opportunity is an earned benefit for both the employee and the organization. It is a clear two-way street.

The organization wants employees who exhibit dependable positive behaviors, share learning, communicate, and collaborate well. The organization wants employees who step forward to identify issues and problems, define them, and offer clear, practical alternatives for resolution. In return, employees want their awareness, experience, and care for the organization to be recognized and rewarded.

The organization wants to have confidence in its flexibility to easily apply its employees' talents easily to meet new challenges as they arise. Employees want to know their capabilities and values are up to the task, and again, they want their talents recognized and rewarded.

Continual Opportunity—What Is It?

Continual opportunity is any activity that expands employees' perspectives of their jobs, departments, capabilities, the application of their interests, and more. Continual opportunity can be:

- Introduction and learning about the functions adjacent to their own job. Meeting the people in those functions and learning how to collaborate better.
- Introduction to sales and spending time with a salesperson to learn what happens in the field.

- Attendance at a trade show relevant to the industry they work in.
- Attending brainstorming sessions in another department.

The list is endless. Every new opening, every new learning expands an employee's perspective, releases the sludge of stagnation, and creates vitality for his or her future.

Next Step?

Release your worn-out perspective of employee incentives. Money and promotion will always be part of the game, but for most of your employees, they are ineffective as incentives. In an age of accelerating change, employees require fundamentally new methods of employee motivation and utilization.

This dramatic paradigm shift demands a redefining of the rules of the game to develop your employees—your key assets—as your new competitive edge.

CHAPTER 14
SUMMARY

"WHAT'S IN IT FOR ME?" INITIALLY CAME AS A SURPRISE TO organizations that traditionally believed that just providing employees with a job with benefits was enough. In this business-as-usual environment, the question "What's in it for me?" came across as harsh, arrogant, and self-serving.

This question actually woke us up. It woke us up to the fact that employees of all ages are learning from social media that success in today's society means continually learning, broadening their awareness and their experience. It means current employees and emerging new talent alike are looking for employers who can offer them more than just a seat within four walls. They may not be able to describe yet what "more" stands for, but they know when it is absent. They know when they are becoming stagnant.

The good thing is you are in the right time, and the right place, to define what "continual opportunity" means for your organization. Offering "more" opportunity and receiving "more" participation is a two-way street. Continual opportunity means establishing clear progressive, personally rewarding incentives for employees—incentives that offer "reach" goals that encourage employees to reach for more opportunity based on their own initiative to learn and participate. Continual opportunity enables employees to earn the right for even more new learning and new opportunities all the time, at their own pace.

Providing progressive opportunity requires Corporate Vitality Team oversight to ensure consistent, systematic provisioning of "What's in it for me?" opportunities for every employee. In today's accelerating business environment, you cannot look the other way and hope employee Vitalization happens. You have to lead it, proactively, always. It has to become a permanent "norm" in your culture.

In the next section, we will address the concept of Integrated Incentives in some depth. Designing, offering and managing Integrated Incentives is elemental to becoming a progressive thinking, learning organization with ever-increasing employee Vitality—employee interest, willingness, ability, and energy to follow you.

NOTES

Actions: _____

_____

_____

_____

_____

Call Whom: _____

_____

_____

_____

_____

By When: _____

_____

_____

_____

_____

"When you're managing a large number of people, you learn that incentives matter tremendously. You really want people to be rewarded for doing the right thing for the customers and the organization."

– RAMEZ NAAM

SECTION 5
THE ENERGIZING POWER OF PROGRESSIVE INCENTIVES

*"Good follow-through doesn't depend on
the right intentions.
It depends on the right incentives."*

– TIMOTHY FERRISS

CHAPTER 15

PROGRESSIVE INCENTIVES CREATE REACH

[Integrated Incentives 1 of 4]

WE ALL NEED TO REACH. IT IS PART OF OUR NATURE. WE WERE born that way.

Everything needs to grow. Without expansion, stagnation and contraction set in. This principle is everywhere. Unfortunately, most businesses ignore this elemental human need for reach. Of the over 2,400 participants in our 2014 inquiry, less than 20 people said their employer offered a proactive incentive program designed to help employees reach further and experience more of their talents and skills. Even fewer said their company encouraged and rewarded the important combination of right behavior and improved performance.

Without incentives, employees stand at a dead end—blocked. They have no place to stretch within your organization, and the unspoken message coming from their leadership is: "We care about your job. We don't care about you." In this setting, even the brightest star will eventually dim. This has a direct effect on all aspects of business, including healthcare costs, turnover rates, and loyalty.

Stagnation affects an employee's quality of work, disposition, and intention. Stagnation filters through all aspects of life.

It doesn't have to be this way.

For some reason, many employers assume their workforce does not need incentives to expand their skills and their reach. The unfortunate result is often a floundering response to unforeseen catastrophes, new opportunities, or sudden market disruptions. Their employees just weren't ready. They were not ready to step into change with new flexible skills and a pro-active can-do attitude.

The Wisdom of a Five-Year-Old Child

Inside every person lives a five-year-old child. What are five year olds interested in? Everything! Everything is new—to see, learn, experience—a new bike, a color, a new ball, or a new song. Every challenge is fun, especially if a reward is involved.

"Without levels of incentives, few will try at all."

If you ask a group of five year olds to hop across a field with a scratchy burlap bag pulled up over their legs, they will—as long as a reward awaits them on the other side. The reward makes all the effort and discomfort worthwhile. For a child, a colorful balloon is a splendid reward, as long as they can see it getting closer to them as they hop.

If you say, "Hop across the field twice, and you'll receive an ice cream cone," some will push for the challenge and some won't. That's the nature of choice.

If you offer an even more significant prize for hopping across the field a third time, fewer will. Some will be satisfied with their ice cream cones. A few will continue to push ahead as long as their strength lasts and the rewards keep growing.

The key point: Without levels of incentives, few will try at all.

Adult employees are no different than those five year olds. Some are happy to stay where they are, left alone and unnoticed. Other employees know they have more to give and feel restrained without new opportunities ahead of them. A few of them ache for even more new challenges to conquer. This internal spark is the shining star—the gift—wrapped into their DNA. It is the same clear energy that makes the grass grow and leaves come out on the trees in the spring. It is inherent in who they are, and there for you if you want to connect.

This intrinsic motivation is unrelated to any level of formal education. These individuals know they have capabilities beyond what they are using at the moment. They know they aren't "just like everyone else."

They need to reach. They need to grow and stretch, to feel more of who they really are, even in the same job.

This essential part of employees is rarely encouraged…and certainly not celebrated. Carefully planned incentives can reach this core need and support every employee, regardless of his or her starting point.

Without reach and nothing to celebrate, eventually good people feel this isn't what they had in mind for their lives. They have no place to go, except home. These people often become the naysayers, the town gossips, and negative influencers as resistors to change.

Is this what you want?

Motivational leadership requires helping employees see ever-new goals. It requires incentives to connect the human need to reach and grow, with the organization's achievement goals.

When this happens, lives become more balanced, interests expand, attitudes improve, and this essential spark begins to glow.

The Incentive Challenge

We see commercial incentives every day—from coupons to dating sites—ranging from single-action incentives to incentives for staying loyal over time. There are fast-response incentives to buy now and layered incentives to "buy more and save more."

Think of a car wash:

- Buy 9 washes, get one free
- Buy 15 washes, get a Light Detail, inside and out for free
- Buy 25 washes, receive a Full Detail for free

Layered incentives generate interest, action, and loyalty, often with immediate gratification as an extra enticement. This is life in the twenty-first century. People are used to it, and expect it.

What do commercial incentives have to do with your organization? A lot. Using this model, you can create powerful reasons for employees to become involved and reach. You can connect employee potential with progressive thinking, learning goals, and opportunities. Without this incentive-reward dynamic, your good talent will look elsewhere for their incentives.

Leaders who understand the impact of meaningful personal incentives create a workforce that stays longer, works harder, and thinks smarter in a state of constant growth. Their employees feel confident in a better future ahead, knowing they will be better able to support their families because they work for you. They feel valued because you help their lights shine brighter than anyone else has.

Tap into Core Emotions

Good incentives relate to how we feel, and how we want to feel. The number one emotion that inspires people is appreciation. Appreciation lifts, motivates, and rewards at the same time. Well-planned incentives convey "I appreciate you" while opening a path of action.

Traditionally, financial increase of any kind and promotion have been the primary incentives, the "carrots" to work harder and give more time. Most employees know both of these are inconsequential for them. Employees know that limited money is allocated for raises and bonuses, and that promotion is almost non-existent and often predetermined.

Even when money is given, the impact is fleeting. Pay raises are generally effective for three months.[35] They have no lasting value. The feeling of value evaporates as the money is spent so its ability to spur employee involvement and vitality is negligible.

Recently, a company in the Western United States learned this the hard way. Hoping to make everyone "happy," it increased everyone's salary to $75,000. After three months, employee interest returned to previous levels, and negativity and poor attitudes remained unresolved. The company did not identify and resolve the issues underlying employee stagnation.

> *"Well-planned incentives provide opportunities for continual reach."*

Well-planned incentives provide opportunities for continual employee reach, the stretch required to raise and expand employee understanding of their own potential. Effective incentives raise self-esteem and self-respect. Well-planned incentives encourage people to come to work because they want to, and to work more diligently with greater collaboration because they want to.

Like any point of influence, these incentives must be directed toward the wants and needs of those receiving them. To do this, it is important to pay attention to the generational diversity among your employees. There are generally three generations in the workforce: Baby Boomers (born 1946-1964), Gen X (born 1965-1982), and Gen Y (a.k.a. Millennials born 1982-2004). All three groups love new experiences, such as adventurous road trips or learning unconventional skills such as gold-panning. They also love flexibility—such as choosing their Friday hours.

Generation Y, now the largest sector within the workforce, is motivated by a constant stream of group information, such as tracking the progress of everyone on the team via an intranet system. Its members expect swift feedback from management as the proof of teamwork. They like constant feedback on how to become better at what they do.[36]

Both Millennials and Boomers place high value on altruism, or giving back. An opportunity to volunteer for a good cause has strong motivational pull. Gaining such an opportunity increases their individual sense of value and becomes an incentive to boost performance on the job.

For example, Pfizer instituted a program called Global Access. Pfizer employees in the global space can get involved in low-cost healthcare for the working poor in countries like Bangladesh. Pfizer partnered with the Grameen Bank on this project, and it became a major recruiting tool. Millennials love the idea that this giant drug company is giving millions in funding, product, and manpower to help those in genuine need. The program's success taps into the altruism[37] of the Gen X, Y, and Z generations.

The challenge is to design meaningful incentive programs that reach employees at an emotional level to increase their productivity at work.

Meaningful Action

With the dramatic increase in negativity and fear in our day-to-day living, we are seeing employee attitudes and confidence decline. Effective leaders must step up to the real responsibility of lifting and reinforcing positive thinking, respectful behavior, and confident skill expansion across the organization. This means taking meaningful action.

What does meaningful action entail? In part, it means helping to:

- Recognize and expand employee potential.
- Provide "reach" incentives that build optimism with greater integrity, insight, and promise.
- Address "What's in it for me?" in a way that builds personal and corporate responsibility.
- Establish a whole-life view of employee training and mentoring.

- Build employees' confidence about prospering in their jobs and supporting their families.
- Reward employees, accelerating employee participation with experiential learning to expand their own flexibility and to increase their contribution for the company.

How do we do this? Luckily, there are clues. The five-year-old child inside everyone is the precedent. A five year old requires:

- Simple, direct, clear, consistent communication
- Timely resolution of issues and problem solving
- Clearly beneficial "whys" ("What's in it for me?")
- The opportunity to experience hands-on learning as well as mentoring
- Consistent behavior expectations
- Clearly defined consequences for poor behavior
- Recognition and celebration

When these are not in place, a five year old becomes touchy when receiving requests, gets angry when ignored, and feels as if he doesn't matter. As an adult, these feelings manifest as negative attitudes, sloppiness, declining responsibility, rejection of accountability, and lower productivity.

However, when these elements are in place, the five year old switches off these tantrums in favor of happy progress toward an exciting goal.

As leaders, your job is to create meaningful action that turns employee lack of interest and malaise into confidence to reach for a better life.

"Expansion of employee perspective is critical."

The Vitality of Possibility is the spark that lights up our spirit with "what ifs." It is the juice that energizes a dream, a challenge to try, and the motivation to be better. Realizing an open door—a new opportunity—can spur us to improve if we listen, learn, and apply ourselves.

The Vitality of Possibility is the catalyst to change employees' perspective from stagnant to curious, then intrigued. Possibilities emerge when employees can see and understand where their jobs fit, why they are important, and what is going on around them. Employees can rarely think "outside the box" they are in unless you help them change the "box" they live in while at work. The more you open and encourage expansion of their perspective about the organization, the more interested and willing to contribute they become.

Some low-cost, low-risk, high-reward ways to help change employee perspectives and help you relate to their possibilities are:

1. **Ask them what they wanted to be when they were five years old:**

   Help them. Ask them to describe what attracted them to this idea. Look within your organization. Find an application for their talents that closely relates to their interests. Connect these dots and you awaken instant interest and vitality.

2. **Ask employees to share their career expectations when they joined your organization:**

   You may find that a significant percentage of employees are in a job they did not ask for and did not want. They accepted a job to help meet the business' needs, only to be left there, forgotten. The closer you can align these employees with their original expectations, the more vitality you will gain.

   > *"Align an employee's job with the employee's interests and watch vitality skyrocket."*

3. **Ask employees about their hobbies and outside interests:**

   A disengaged employee sees her job as an unavoidable distraction until she can put the bulk of her energy and wisdom into what she loves to do. Why not tap into this secret power center by applying what she loves to do in your organization in some way?

   This might call for adjusting the scope or purpose of the employee's job, or applying her natural talents in a different area altogether. "What's in it for me?" connects employees to meaningful assignments that enable employees to use their natural talents where they can excel and have fun in the process. This is vitality!

   Align your employee's interests to needs within your organization and watch morale and loyalty skyrocket.

CASE STUDY
FRANK[38]

Frank was a surly, standoffish guy in the accounting department, the overweight grouch who sat in the third cubical to the left pouring over actuarial spreadsheets in stolid silence. Every morning, his fellow employees would arrive to greet their curmudgeon mascot with "Good morning, Frank!" and hear his familiar grunt in reply.

His supervisors respected his work and generally left him alone.

A friendly intern named Joe watched this process and decided to make a difference in Frank's life. He started by asking Frank general questions about the day, or his ride to work, and sometimes brought him a cup of coffee. Frank would shift uneasily, mumble something, wave his hand in some form of oblique courtesy, and go back to work.

Joe kept this up for weeks. Slowly, he made progress in communicating with Frank. While others were at lunch, Joe would sit nearby with a homemade sandwich and talk to Frank. Joe asked about the work. He asked for Frank's insight on the organization. He invited Frank's opinion on opportunities for a young cost accountant in training.

Slowly, the conversation became more open. Joe discovered that Frank had been in the same seat doing the same work for twenty years. Frank's perspective was clear. The business was okay, but the management had no interest in listening to the employees' ideas. Management wanted employees to sit in their chairs, with mouths and minds closed, and be glad for their jobs. Frank had given up long ago.

Management had no other use for him, so he had no use for them. "I just do my work and go home," he told Joe.

During one of their lunchtime dialogues, Joe noticed some photos of young children on Frank's desk, hidden away from general office view. This seemed contrary to the persona Frank projected at work, so Joe gently inquired about the children.

Frank turned slowly to look at the pictures, and after a long silent pause, he said, "These are my grandchildren. They live across the country in California." Frank's voice sounded gentle and kind, a completely different side to Frank than Joe had ever seen.

"Do you travel to see them often?" Joe asked.

Frank shook his head. "I've never been out there. It's too far, and it costs too much. We talk on Skype every Sunday night." He went on to tell about his grandchildren—three boys ages four, five, and seven. The boys enjoyed their bikes and loved school. Frank's face softened into the hint of a smile when he spoke about their young dreams for their lives.

This was the opening Joe was hoping for. "What about you, Frank?" Joe asked. "What did you want to do when you were that age?"

Frank's face lit up. "I always wanted to be a fireman." He chuckled a little sheepishly and rubbed his meaty jaw.

"So did I!" Joe said. "I saw myself climbing on the roof and hacking through it to put the fire hose inside the house. What about you?"

"I wanted to be the guy who drove the truck, red lights flashing, going at breakneck speed to save the day."

Joe blinked. Frank wanted to be a hero, in the middle of the action. No wonder Frank was surly and kept to himself. Every day, all day long, for years, he had been disconnected from his dreams and talents. No one knew him or cared. Frank was stagnant.

Thousands of "Franks" are everywhere. Disengaged., with stagnating interests, ignored talents, angry, and frustrated. Does that mean the supervisor should transfer Frank to a Firehouse? Not at all. But think of the nature of a firehouse. What comes to mind? Doing something that helps people, fast moving, constant changes, teamwork, and of course, the color red.

Frank's employer didn't have to change Frank's profession. He could do accounting anywhere. What was the solution? He was moved to an active sales office where he could engage both his heart and his accounting expertise to help solve customer problems. The office already contained aspects of the life Frank desired. His supervisor placed a picture of a red fire engine in his office and said his job was to put out fires and build relationships with customers.

Frank thrived. His surliness vanished, and his health improved. He volunteered to participate on problem-solving teams, volunteered to work longer hours, and became a major asset to the company.

The supervisor changed the "box" for Frank, and his contribution multiplied.

This true story is a wonderful example of a person who seemed to be a negative personality but who was actually misplaced and miserable. By asking questions and listening, this situation turned around to the benefit of everyone.

CHAPTER 15
SUMMARY

OF THE OVER 2,400 PARTICIPANTS IN OUR STUDY, LESS THAN twenty said their employer offered an incentive program designed to help employees expand their talents and skills. Even fewer said their company rewarded improved performance. When an organization has no incentives, it is saying to its employees, "We don't care if you stay where you are." This unspoken message leads to stagnation.

Neither money nor promotion are effective incentives until an employee rises above a critical management level. Meaningful incentives help employees feel a new confidence in their ability to contribute to the organization and their future.

Progressive leaders recognize and expand employee potential through incentives that address "What's in it for me?" across generational lines, cultural lines, and at every level of the company. They also reward employee participation. This active recognition for who they are as well as what they do increases energy, interest, enthusiasm, and participation. Loyalty grows with opportunities. Employees become fully present and involved.

NOTES

Actions: _____

_____

_____

_____

_____

Call Whom: _____

_____

_____

_____

_____

By When: _____

_____

_____

_____

_____

*"Employees who believe that management
is concerned about them as a whole person
—not just an employee—
are more productive, more satisfied, more fulfilled."*

– ANNE M. MULCAHY

CHAPTER 16

A LIVING FABRIC OF INCENTIVES

[Integrated Incentives 2 of 4]

THE CONCEPT OF INTEGRATED INCENTIVES HONORS employees for both who they are, what they do now, and for their potential. A Living Fabric of Incentives combines progressive learning and support, mentoring, recognition, and celebration. It provides continual incentive, not once-a-year enticement. It is a FLOW of learning and opportunities that enhances interest, vitality, and real commitment in an organization.

Developing Integrated Incentives requires changing their paradigm from considering incentives as an afterthought or an extra expense, offered occasionally or as the budget permits, to a highly valued, ongoing, high quality process to increase employee value through their awareness, skills, interest, and application.

A Living Fabric of Incentives is not a one-size-fits-all program, nor is it a fixed curriculum. Unlike traditional on-site or online eLearning delivery systems, a living fabric of incentives provides employees with opportunities to expand their perspectives about the business and participate in progressive experiential learning with mentoring while working in their current jobs. It enables employees to evolve continually at their own rates, respecting their different levels of personal incentive. It enables employees with high personal incentive and natural people skills to shine, accelerating their learning and contributions, regardless of education level. This continual introduction to new learning and opportunity builds employees' confidence that they will no longer be stagnant and that your company has their best interests in mind.

Some leaders ask: "Will we lose control? Will we lose our ability to manage numbers and create reports? How will we maintain consistent productivity?"

The answer is you will not lose control. On the contrary, you have even more control through more communication and collaboration, and more awareness of what's really happening in your organization. By creating an environment where employees have more incentive, they require *less* control and will take on more responsibility.

Gap? What Gap?

A clear framework to Vitalize Your Workforce includes sincere inquiry about employees' interests, natural skills, talents, and hobbies. When this inquiry is followed by questions about their work experience to date in your organization, you can easily see a gap between what they really have to offer and what they are actually using. When you understand this gap, you can use it as a starting point for your mentoring, and you can create a plan to fill that gap and begin to enlist their curiosity and willingness to participate.

Meaningful Training

Meaningful Training engages employees in new skills and experiences that are valuable for work, at home, and within their communities. It expands employee perspectives of where their job fits into your organization and why it is important, while building interest and Vitality.

Meaningful training moves away from the idea of training as an occasional day to attend a course that may or may not apply to your business.

Meaningful training requires active employee participation in learning with hands-on experience in issue resolution, problem solving, solution development, and how to offer recommendations. No matter what their position, people need to know how to work together to solve problems anytime, anywhere, and to collaborate on new ideas.

Meaningful training helps people listen more effectively, gives them tools, and stimulates their desire to collaborate. It encourages those with natural leadership skills to step forward anywhere in the organization at any time.

Meaningful training intentionally expands the employee's perspective. Through shared-learning in critical skills as collaborative problem solving, delegation, and mentoring, each employee slowly learns more about the organization, how departments connect to each other, how to solve problems within that framework, how to recommend improvements, and how to increase their contribution effectively.

Meaningful training also includes encouraging employees to teach and apply these skills at home and in their communities. These are important opportunities to practice the new capabilities, to help deepen constructive ideas, positive thinking, and actions for people everywhere. Give employees credit and recognition for volunteering to teach these principles at community clubs, places of worship, Boy Scouts, job core, or when coaching a sports team and watch their confidence rise.

Teaching others what they are learning helps deepen their own understanding of what they are teaching and instills the great need others have to learn it too. Importantly, this teaching at home and in their communities provides increased practice and hands-on experience that accelerates the employees' ability to contribute more effectively at work.

The Importance of Choice

A major factor in this program's success is choice—the permission for employees to choose to stay where they are, or to participate in Vitalizing Your Workforce shared-learning programs. This choice in effect, shares the responsibility for evolving your workforce from stagnant to vital, with the employees themselves. Choice means employees understand that development of their own perspectives and potential is a pro-active shared responsibility, a win-win for everyone, not just the organization.

Choice means that all employees can participate regardless of age or education, to increase their value to the organization. The more participation, the greater their increase in personal self-esteem and confidence. The greater their increase in self-esteem and confidence, the greater their opportunities and contribution.

Choice also means that non-participation is a viable option. Choice honors employees who are happy with their current jobs and positions and just want to stay where they are. That is okay. Let these employees know that the choice is theirs any time. When they want to participate further, they simply communicate their desire and go! In the meantime, simply clarify that they will continue to be rewarded with business-as-usual rewards.

This choice also means that new boundaries and consequences for negativity and complaining about the job can now be established. These boundaries and consequences can be easily included in your Vitalized Corporate Policy statement.

Previously, negative and complaining employees were difficult to remove. Now the game is changed, permanently. Those who choose not to participate in enhancing their potential and contribution cannot complain about their current jobs and the workplace. If they continue to be negative, that is also their choice. This choice opens up a conversation about their options and facilitates release. No more waiting months to build a defensible "HR File" for change or removal.

Corporate Vitality Team Oversight

Just implementing programs for continual employee learning and opportunity is a big step, but it's not enough. You must ensure that the continual learning opportunities go in a direction, that they mean something—they add up to new openings, new opportunities to help build employee confidence and participation.

Instituting a tracking system for continual learning and opportunity helps:

- ensure every employee who wants to be included, is included.
- ensure all managers are participating in their dedicated people-leadership programs.
- raise awareness when more individual mentoring is required.
- provide recognition and celebration.
- recognition of when employees are ready for new assignments.

This system, managed with intention by the Corporate Vitality Team, helps encourage employees to reach for expansion of their own future every day, while working for you—and knowing they have support.

CHAPTER 16
SUMMARY

INTEGRATED INCENTIVES HONOR EMPLOYEES FOR WHO they are, what they do now, and for their potential. Developing Integrated Incentives means taking a fresh look at employee-incentive programs. It means changing their paradigm from an afterthought or an extra expense to a highly valued, ongoing program for employee evolution.

Employee choice to participate is a key element to establishing clear joint responsibility for the expansion of employee perspectives and capabilities.

Integrated Incentives combine multiple avenues for ongoing progressive experience, learning and support, providing continual opportunity for employee reach.

Integrated Incentives include meaningful training that moves away from the idea of training as an occasional day to attend a course that may or may not apply to your business. Meaningful training requires active employee participation in learning with hands-on experience in critical skill areas such as collaborative issue resolution and problem solving.

Implementing programs for continual employee learning and opportunity also requires oversight to ensure that the continual learning opportunities go in a direction, that they mean something…they add up to new openings, new opportunities to help build employee confidence and participation. This oversight is a leading role for your Corporate Vitality Team.

NOTES

Actions: _____

_____

_____

_____

_____

_____

Call Whom: _____

_____

_____

_____

_____

_____

By When: _____

_____

_____

_____

_____

_____

*"Customers will never love a company
until the employees love it first."*

– SIMON SINEK

CHAPTER 17

CREATING AND MANAGING INTEGRATED INCENTIVES

[Integrated Incentives 3 of 4]

WHEN DESIGNING AN INCENTIVE PLAN, IT IS BEST AND easiest to adopt a format, a model, that is easily recognized and accepted by employees from the loading dock to the corner office. Choose a model that is already proven across cultures and regions, and adaptable to any situation and industry.

It is also imperative that the model for incentives easily and quickly imparts different levels of achievement to attain, what behaviors and actions are required to attain those levels, and what rewards are available at each level. Importantly, the model must be simple enough for all employees to understand, both the premise for—and its promise.

"The credit card model speaks without words."

The Credit Card Model

The credit card model is a layered incentive approach that most of the world's population recognizes. Its use of color quickly conveys levels of benefit, enhances interest, and engages participation. In essence, the credit card model speaks without words, simultaneously connecting and offering various levels of incentive appeal.

The Vitalize Integrated Incentives program purposefully introduces the idea of the credit card model to describe progressive levels of action and reward. This model immediately instills the value of increased opportunity for employees—to do more, become more, contribute more, gain more—if they take action. From there, the tiered model quickly expands from a fixed (limited) number of tiers to a progressive pathway for each individual in the organization.

Using our new paradigm for Integrated Incentives, employees have an at-a-glance view of: 1) where they are now, 2) the different levels of opportunity, 3) the actions and behaviors they must exhibit to reach them, and 4) the rewards attainable at each step. You can customize the desired behaviors and actions you wish to foster; define the rewards, and lead to the next step opportunities associated with those rewards. These choices are up to you.

Whatever you choose, define meaningful, progressive achievement levels, requirements, and opportunities for your employees to increase their value to themselves and for your organization. Be clear and consistent, and communicate to all employees. Remember, we are on a quest to release stagnation everywhere in the organization. Past management practices were designed to be selective, be in control, and enable singling out of an individual here or there for promotion, often with poorly defined criteria. The majority of employees were in the dark about the selection's why or how.

The quantum leap now is to teach and reward progressive thinking employees who learn and exemplify Vitality Principals. This is your new competitive edge. *Your* job is to lead for Vitality throughout the organization. Once you set the Vitality engine in motion, keep it revved! Reinforce it with clearly communicated Vitality programs, opportunities, and rewards. Transformation from stagnant to Vitality will begin slowly because stagnant employees don't expect anything new from you. Once they see it, hear it, and believe it, your vision and leadership will become clear and employees will begin to meet your pace.

Vitality Learning Opportunities Are Unlimited

Vitality opportunities can be new skill development, introduction to other departments, or auditing a problem-solving sessions in other departments. Auditing other problem-solving sessions can reinforce how to apply the Vitalize Issue Resolution Process anytime, anywhere, and importantly, how to consider the impact of decisions on other job functions.

Opportunity rewards can include cross-training and mentoring in adjacent functions or in new areas of greater interest to the employee. Cross-training and shared learning enables employees to learn about other department's goals, issues, resolutions, and successes. This learning broadens their understanding of the organization and the importance of their own job. Hearing other employees participate builds their own confidence, improves their ability to speak up, and increases collaboration.

Progressive thinking learning organizations know that the effect of annual reviews for promotion or salary increase (alone or in combination) are not effective incentives for most employees. Yes, promotion and salary increase is a required standard procedure in an organization, but new criteria for these awards must be defined and required for clear, focused, exemplary Vitality Leadership expertise.

Vitality attitudes, behaviors, actions, and people-leadership skills must be instilled as leadership requirements from the bottom up. When you foster Vitality leadership everywhere in your organization, and employees know that new actions and behaviors are required and mentored, they pay attention. With this new freedom, employees understand they can expand their careers at any time, based on their own initiatives and potential. When employees activate the power of choice and feel the Vitality of Possibility, they apply increased energy for their own progress—while working for you. They can see the future value of their own efforts. This is a cornerstone for Vitality!

Sequential Performance

Utilizing well-defined, progressive performance goals with associated actions educates employees and guides them to sequential learning, action, greater contribution, and greater reward. For instance, learning and becoming proficient in the principles and processes for Vitalize Issue Resolution and Problem Solving can open the door to learning about and joining other departments' problem-solving initiatives. That step can open the door to experiencing Customer Service functions, thus resolving customer issues. This step can then open the door to auditing a new product development team exploring possible future issues to address, then open to an opportunity in Vitality Leadership mentoring of Core Skills. These are all very real opportunities that expand perspective, build confidence, and increase the ability to contribute more.

Why learn & practice Core Skills?

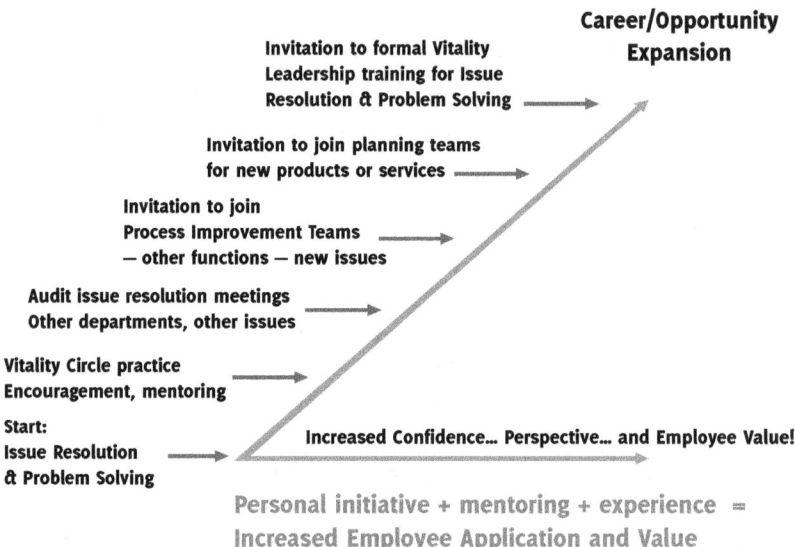

Personal initiative + mentoring + experience =
Increased Employee Application and Value

Permission and Encouragement

Employees generally don't know how to improve their performances on their own. Simply asking people to improve their performances on their own without guidance, mentoring, and incentive has little effect.

Why? Most employees don't see the bigger picture of their jobs or organizations to know which actions will result in improved productivity and recognition. Although some people will do their best as a part of their basic character, most need guidance to stretch out of their comfort zones, learn something new, and feel valuable in the process. Remember the five-year-old child? The principles are the same.

With effective planning and progressive incentives, employees will easily align with Vitality generating cross-training, shared learning, and mentoring programs. This winning combination helps employees become comfortable with new tasks and behaviors, and increases their willingness to accept a greater personal vision for themselves.

Baseline—Standard Performance

Establishing and respecting a Basic Standard Performance Level forms your baseline. Every incentive program needs a starting point—a baseline, a performance description that applies to employees who are either just entering the organization or existing employees who provide good work, are happy with their current jobs, and have no need or interest to move on. Employees at this level contribute significantly to your organization's current stability. It is important that they be proud of their work and feel appreciated and recognized for their consistent dedication to the organization.

Learning the new required Vitalize Core Skills at this level provides continual new thought. These core skills include: Vitalize Issue Resolution and Problem Solving, Dynamic Delegation, and Mentoring. It enables any employee to listen and participate differently anywhere, any time. They expand the employee's awareness and belief in your new vision for a Vitalized Culture for the organization.

The Standard Performance learning of Vitalize Core Skills also requires practice. The generation of at least two recommendations for problem or process-improvements in any area every year ensures understanding of the Core Skill, facilitates skill development, and increases confidence. It continually reminds these employees there is room to grow at their own pace, and that the choice is theirs—not mandated by the organization. They can also choose to participate in the expanded progressive learning Vitalize Program for new opportunity at any time, or stop participating at any time depending on their learning speed or interest level, without retribution. Employee choice is a powerful tool for employee satisfaction and loyalty.

Medium Level Participation

Employees who are proactive, demonstrating personal initiative and applying themselves to the Vitalize Progressive Learning program, gain significant opportunity advantage. In addition to introduction to different departments and functions, the employee can audit other problem-solving sessions, and learn to participate in new product or service brainstorming activities. Google requires all employees to attend brainstorming sessions of other departments, whether they are familiar with that department or not. This attendance is instrumental in expanding their employees' perspective and confidence in a highly practical way, and it provides them with awareness of future skills and opportunity rewards available to them.

Advanced or High-Level Opportunity Rewards

Employees who demonstrate high initiative with required behaviors and actions for leadership gain additional Core Skill training for Vitality people-leadership. These skills must be honed and proven for future promotion. The Advanced or Progressive Path requires providing at least four recommendations for problem or process improvement in any area within each year to ensure understanding, practice, advanced skill development, and application.

Individuals taking steps along the Progressive Path receive greater business and leadership skill training. Leadership skill training might include the opportunity to collaborate in process improvements, developing product or service ideas, or joining profit-cost dialogue.

Employees may meet executives; audit business reviews; gain experience in research, in-field sales and sales meetings, report writing, presentation creation and delivery; and participate proactively in visible people-leadership communication.

Advancing on the Progressive Path requires providing at least six recommendations for problem or process improvement in any area within the year. This requirement enhances observation skills and abilities to communicate effectively with management, and it expands cross-organization thinking. Importantly, it also includes hands-on experience and practice of leadership behaviors for greater Vitalize People-Leadership responsibility.

Note: Practicing "leadership behaviors" does not mean people have to become leaders. Many people do not want to be leaders. However, a lot of people would like to work around or work for leaders. The more experience they have in all the aspects of leadership, the more open and progressive their thinking and contributions can be, even behind the scenes.

So, what is different from the standard salary and once-a-year promotion review so prevalent today? Vitalize embeds rewarding the employee with a new experiential opportunity any time of year, based on their personal initiative and proven interest and participation. There are steps, behaviors, actions, and participation tracking to ensure recognition and reward for the employee that are beneficial to his or her individual career as well as the business.

Natural People-Leaders Shine

Your natural people-leaders are the gold nuggets who will emerge within your organization now that they have permission and encouragement to do so. They want more people-leadership opportunity. When given the chance, natural people-leaders stand tall with personal initiative to learn and gain more and more experience regardless of their level or lack of formal education.

Progressive thinking, learning organizations recognize the unlimited value of these sterling individuals. They treasure and mentor them, involving them as part of the company's new vertical and horizontal employee-communication network.

Rewards further expand the perspectives of these Vitalized employees. Perhaps they can join meetings in other locations, or attend off-site meetings with customers, or support a trade show. These employees become involved in more mentoring for themselves and for others.

In an office, such a reward can involve introducing the employee to the logistics of running an office, including an introduction to the different accounting functions, insurance resolutions, time tracking, and key issues to address for business expansion.

If the company has day and night shifts, the employee can join process improvements efforts to improve the handoff between shifts and train new employees. All of these experiences help open the employee's perspective to become a greater contributor to the office and in his or her own life.

Introduce these employees to strategic thinking and planning within the organization. Perhaps the employee can attend different meetings or discussions, take on a research project, or join decision analysis teams. All of these areas expand awareness and open the perspective for opportunity.

Employees with high personal incentive who want to learn and earn Vitality Leadership and increase their contributions to the business can ask and receive more advanced skill development. This introduces more formal mentoring in how to think about a whole organization, how to handle difficult situations, and how to make decisions. It could include introduction and exposure to external team members perhaps, such as auditing or product sourcing.

Training may include enabling an employee to participate in some aspect of strategic planning for the coming year, or track goal attainment for the quarter. Elemental to this step is the origination of at least nine suggestions for improvement, or three larger problem-solving opportunities.

These rewards promote upward visibility and formal training in a functional area of their choice, a customized training program toward a certification or degree program, or an internship with a Vitality leader.

CHAPTER 17
SUMMARY

INTEGRATED INCENTIVES ARE A FLOW[39] OF OPPORTUNITY for the employee along a progressive path to Vitalization. They are a living fabric of incentives that provide continual opportunity for the employee in a progressive, meaningful way that expands employee perspective, experience, training, mentoring, and opportunity. The Vitalize Integrated Incentives plan respects each individual for the skills and education they have at the moment, while systematically providing the choice to learn, expand, and contribute more.

The Vitalize Integrated Incentives model starts with identifying and respecting the starting point or baseline for each employee. This baseline is call the Standard Performance Level. Some employees are content to stay at this level. This is a conscious choice that requires respect, with the knowledge that they will receive the Standard Rewards for their choice.

Each step taken with personal initiative offers increased training, introduction to more areas of the company, more exposure to leadership, and more mentoring. Each step also has increasing requirements for issue resolution and problem solving, pro-active mentoring for skill and knowledge transfer, increased collaboration, increased exposure to management functions, and Vitality Leadership.

The opportunity to partake in increasing levels of shared learning and opportunity is dependent on the individual employees' personal incentive and level of proactive participation. The employee can earn more and more opportunity—discovering and increasing his "why?" Employees with high interest and those who are natural people-leaders can accelerate at their own paces regardless of their starting points or educational backgrounds. This is a significant win-win for the employees and the organization. This is Vitality!

All employees want increased confidence that they can support their families and that the organization cares about them, as individuals and for their work. They want increased confidence in their ability to do more, be more—while working for you. Integrated Incentives provide a consistent, sustainable framework for both employee and company evolution to a progressive thinking, learning organization with Vitality to meet accelerating market opportunity and change.

NOTES

Actions: _____

_____

_____

_____

_____

Call Whom: _____

_____

_____

_____

_____

By When: _____

_____

_____

_____

_____

"Always treat your employees exactly as you want them to treat your best customers."

– STEPHEN R. COVEY

CHAPTER 18

MEANINGFUL REWARDS CREATE LOYALTY

[Integrated Incentives 4 of 4]

CLEAR, MEANINGFUL REWARDS PROVIDE A LASTING incentive. Meaningful rewards create loyalty. They connect with the employee on both an emotional level and a practical level.

"Meaningful rewards do not have to be costly or complicated."

Meaningful rewards do not have to be costly or complicated. They need to be real, thoughtful, and evolve with the employee. What is important for one employee at a point in time is not necessarily valuable for another.

Take time to find out what is meaningful to each employee. It is not hard to find out, and you might be surprised by the answers. Set up a schedule of inquiries with each employee. Ask each one what rewards, what personal rewards are most meaningful at this point in his or her life. What will encourage him or her to provide more time, diligence, and effort? This dialogue can benefit both you and the employee for many reasons, and generate great loyalty in the process.

Some employees might feel that assuring their childcare payment is paid on time is an important reward. Others might feel contribution or service to help care for an elder, or to a grandchild's education is important. These rewards can be budgeted and offered through alternative accounting structures other than through salary and bonus and still be of high importance to the employee.

Part of the reward is the human-ness, the care for employees' well-being rather than just a remote distribution of funds by a system that doesn't even know their names. Thinking about and addressing their current needs is not welfare thinking. It is part of a progressive thinking, learning organization that values and demonstrates flexibility in caring for its employees.

The inquiry relative to preferred reward can take place during hiring, during performance reviews, or during one-on-one conversations between the employee and his or her supervisor. Ask employees directly, which rewards might be important to them over the next twelve months; then provide solutions to help fill their needs.

Inquiry into current needs for each employee requires interest and gentle two-way communication. When the conversation is managed with sincerity, not just checking a box, it provides a gateway for regular communication, and a positive reminder for the employee throughout the year that you are paying attention to his needs.

As you create a list of personal rewards that are meaningful to most of your employees, you can aggregate the findings and create a list of rewards that are possible for you offer. You can determine the most efficient way of offering those benefits, and provide the selection to your employees to choose which is most beneficial to them at this time. Many firms offering meaningful-reward initiatives find that creating and offering services in-house at cost is actually more helpful for both the organization and employee than funding commercial services provided at a distance from work.

> *"Meaningful rewards show employees that their organization cares."*

The top-rated TV show *Undercover Boss*[40] manages a version of this approach quite effectively. The CEO develops each employee reward through personal inquiry into the employee's situation and finding the driving need in his or her life. What does the employee need that will help release stuck energy from his or her life so the employee can be freer to contribute more at work?

A meaningful rewards program shows employees that their organization cares. It recognizes and communicates that the employee's contribution is both important and recognized; and that if she continues to exemplify the company's values, expanded opportunities await her in the future. Although *Undercover Boss* rewards only four or five employees at a time (on the show), the same principles can be applied more expansively in any organization.

As an employee's needs are not consistent year after year, an annual check-in renews the personal dialogue and allows the reward to evolve with the employee. This can easily become another aspect of a progressive thinking, learning organization that understands and demonstrates Vitality.

Meaningful Benefits as Appreciation and Recognition

Earlier, we emphasized the importance of appreciation and recognition as meaningful incentives for expansion of employee learning and effort. Meaningful rewards are easily offered as grateful appreciation and recognition for employee contribution.

"Appreciation is sincere acknowledgment of work well done."

Appreciation is the catalyst, the human electricity. It is the feeling that inspires people to do more. It is the "juice" that gives people permission to feel good about themselves and be open to learning.

Providing a meaningful reward, perhaps a payment for school as a "thank you," has great value for the recipient. The challenge today is how to create a method of appreciation that is not so fleeting that it becomes meaningless and self-serving in the rush of the workday. Saying "Thanks! I appreciate that!" and walking away is momentary and holds little meaning. The more this habit is repeated, the less meaning it conveys. When expressed sincerely in a way that is lasting to the recipient, balance is created. For instance, when an employee offers a service or a kindness, the recipient can help with something in return, or make an extra effort by offering a thank you in writing and placing the acknowledgment in the employee's personal Appreciation File.

Educate and Share while Recognizing

Effective communication of achievement is an art. When recognizing someone for his or her effort, make it a learning opportunity for the audience. Teach the audience what the person who is receiving the recognition did to gain the acknowledgment. First, explain the problem as it was before the employee took action. Next, describe the employee's steps to resolve the situation. Then, be clear on how the employee improved the situation.

This approach takes two minutes or less. It is a no-cost, low-risk, high-reward practice of progressive thinking organizations that see every moment as a mentoring opportunity. Most employees thirst for information on how to improve themselves for greater return. Shared recognition and reward has significant "stickiness." It helps develop a sense of self-esteem, builds confidence, adds Vitality to the employee's sense of future possibility, and can last for years.

Please note that it is important to respect how each employee prefers to be recognized. Some people like to be in the limelight. Some people prefer to stay in the background. More reticent employees prefer one-on-one acknowledgment with a thoughtfully written description of what they did placed into their Appreciation File. This action has a long-term reward too.

As simple as it sounds, a Thank You letter written in the problem-action-result format on organization letterhead, signed by the head of the department or the CEO, is also both visible and lasting. The letter can be offered in a frame and hung in the employee's office, or on a wall at home for others to see. It can be part of a newsletter, and it can be carefully saved for use during evaluation periods or when interviewing for a position inside or outside your organization. This is highly beneficial for the employee and low cost.

CHAPTER 18
SUMMARY

TRADITIONAL EMPLOYEE BENEFITS SUCH AS HEALTHCARE and insurance will always be necessary. Carefully defined meaningful benefits and rewards can be highly effective as employee incentives, and they can be relatively low cost and easy to deliver. Meaningful rewards are real, thoughtful, usually solve a problem, or support a primary interest of the employee.

Meaningful rewards as incentives evolve with the employee. What is important for one employee at a point in time in his life, is not necessarily valuable for another. Some employees might value free childcare. Others might value a contribution to their grandchild's education. Part of the reward's value is the company's care for employee wellbeing. The top-rated TV show *Undercover Boss* manages a version of this approach quite effectively.

Each reward stems from personal inquiry into the employee's situation. An annual conversation renews this personal dialogue and enables the selection of a reward that evolves with the employee, meeting his or her new needs in a new year.

Shared recognition offered with sincere education and appreciation can be an effective incentive too. Communicating an achievement well is an art. When recognizing someone for his or her effort, if you make it a learning opportunity for the audience, and share the achievement with others, the benefit can be lasting.

NOTES

Actions: _____

_____

_____

_____

_____

Call Whom: _____

_____

_____

_____

_____

By When: _____

_____

_____

_____

_____

"Change is inevitable, growth is intentional."
– GLENDA CLOUD

SECTION 6
TAKE CHARGE

"Strong leadership is essential to instill and manage for Vitality."

– JAMES ROBERTSON

CHAPTER 19

INTRODUCING A CHIEF VITALITY OFFICER POSITION[41]

THIS IS A NEW ERA WITH NEW REQUIREMENTS FOR CRITICAL leadership. As an organization dependent on people as your key asset, it is time to focus on an executive level officer whose specified job is to increase and sustain the organization's Vitality.

The time is past for employees to be counted only as numbers, or to be regarded as just the job or seat they sit in. That management approach worked through the 1990s when computer access to comparative salary treatments, alternative job opportunities, and the Millennial cry for "What's in it for me?" did not exist. Now it does. Add the advent of the internet, mobile, big data, unlimited computer capacity, bandwidth, and more. The whole game changed—permanently.

The whole outer game changed, but within organizations, very few companies recognized the need to change the *inner* game to become a progressive thinking, learning organization.

Research about employee lack of engagement has been around for over twenty years, but we now know—most research was asking the wrong questions. The resulting solutions had low, short-lived impact. Hierarchical top-down leadership with closed agendas continued through 2015. Employee value was acknowledged but not developed as a primary asset, and the ability to lead increasingly disgruntled employees disintegrated daily.

Millennials joined the ranks introducing "What's in it for me?" and they meant it. If they didn't see a future or at least a near-term opportunity for themselves—out they went. At a replacement cost of 30-60 percent or more of annual salary for entry level employees, 150 percent of annual salary for mid-level employees, this budget line item began to hurt. When Boomers and union workers took up the "What's in it for me?" chant, the budget line broke as did the ability to direct and lead these employees to do more for the sake of the company.

Employees became more and more discouraged and remote. Remedies to make employees "happier" started to emerge. Facilitating day care closer to work is a very good thing. It solves a lot of employee worry. Flex hours and more work from home are very beneficial for many employees. And yes, more training is important.

So, what is the problem? Why do we need yet another executive leader to take charge as a Chief Vitality Officer? Because the world has become exponentially more complex, technology is exponentially faster with applications seeding every minute, competition can build a market or interrupt one overnight—yet the way organizations protect and evolve their employee talents has *not* kept up.

You say, "So? Why a Chief Vitality Officer?"

The need to raise employees out of the sludge and malaise of personal stagnation and resignation (not caring about you or your company anymore) is mandatory. Personal stagnation of employees, in the face of young entrepreneurs making millions on the internet while still in their teens, affects more and more employees than ever before. Frustration and resentment run high, internal sabotage is on the rise, and damaging company reputation on the outside is rising too.

If left unattended, this situation may damage a company's ability to respond effectively to even a small calamity or opportunity. In time, it may actually destroy the company too.

"How about Human Resources?" you say. "Why not assign the job to them?" Because the training, skills, and responsibilities of an HR executive versus a Chief Vitality Officer are vastly different. Human Resources employees are specialists, among many other things, in federal and state rules and regulations for hiring, firing, administering health benefits, vacation, time off, helping employees manage challenges and calamities at work and at home, and diversity management. Their focus is different, and their measurement system for success is different. (Note: Many Human Resource executives and practitioners are striving to become greater motivational leaders for an organization. Vitalize Your Workforce will help in this endeavor and we welcome working with you. Transforming stagnation to Vitality will require action from all of us.)

The Chief Vitality Officer is a different talent altogether. Let's take a look:

Critical Characteristics of a Chief Vitality Officer[42]

The following characteristics were generated via a formal systematic survey and analysis process. The percentages provide the relative weighted value of each characteristic. They are listed from the most important to the least important characteristics.

1. **Intuits Vitalize—18 percent**

    Has a natural intuitive grasp of the Vitalize Principles and Methods for Vitalizing the Workforce, and has an intense commitment to implement them company-wide.

2. **Empowered Executive—17 percent**

    Is a full C-Level Executive who sits at the top table with very close ties to the CEO. The organization's overall functioning rests ultimately with the CEO. The Chief Vitality Officer must report directly to the CEO where decisions can be made to enhance the whole organization's performance. Any assignment of this role to less than executive level will be ignored and ineffective.

3. **Visionary Leader—16 percent**

    Is passionate about his or her vital role as a critical leader for Vitality in the organization. A visionary leader whose goal is to identify and release stagnation anywhere it exists in the organization, transforming it into positive proactive employee energy that is flexible, aware, expanding, and loyal. An excellent communicator with proven collaboration, organization, planning, and implementation skills.

4. **Effective Leader—15 percent**

   Is a strong, proven, decisive, and empathetic leader.

5. **Drives Strategic Essence—14 percent**

   Possesses a deep understanding of the organization's strategic essence and a clear view of how to maximize it.

6. **People are *the* Greatest Asset—10 percent**

   Sees people in the organization as intensely valuable and passionately desires to enable them to reach their full potential in support of the organization's strategic goals.

7. **Results Oriented—10 percent**

   Has a focused, persistent, strong ability to get things done.

Critical Functions of the Chief Vitality Officer[43]

The Chief Vitality Officer is a C-level executive with a powerful vision of how to unleash the workforce's full potential, develop sustainable Vitality Leadership, and develop a Culture of Vitality and capability across the enterprise.

1. **Listening—20 percent**

   Listens to the heart of the organization—employee and management combined. Has his or her finger on the pulse—the essence and health—of the organization. Knows the depth of stagnation in key areas of the business, develops programs to release that stagnation and create sustainable Vitality.

2. **Oversees the Vitalize Integrated Employee Incentive Program—17 percent**

   Designs, implements, and administers the Vitalize Integrated Employee Incentive Program for the company. Instills new employee vitality goals, and customizes actions and behaviors that serve as continual reach goals for employees to earn new learning, expanded participation, and new work opportunities for themselves.

3. **Measures—16 percent**

   Oversees application of the Corporate Vitality Assessment Suite[44] of Measurement Tools. Maintains a rolling assessment schedule and data reporting to the C-level team, board of directors, managers, and individuals.

4. **Oversees Cross-Training and Shared Learning—12 percent**

   - Oversees the implementation and management of employee critical skill evolution required for transformation to a Vitalized organization. Among others, Employee Programs include:
     - Vitalize Issue Resolution and Problem Solving
     - Vitalize Dynamic Delegation
     - Vitalize Universal Mentoring
     - Vitalize Integrated Incentives
     - Vitalize Active Appreciation
     - Vitalize Recognition and Celebration
     - Vitalize Personal Opportunity Development
   - Designs, implements, and manages a quality employee participation tracking system to ensure positive, progressive learning of news skills and opportunity development for every employee.
   - Designs, oversees, and tracks management training for Vitality Leadership to ensure people-leaders are in place, implementing Vitalize Programs in their departments.
   - Works with HR to ensure alignment of Vitality Leadership and employee transformation with other formal employee HR reporting programs. Interfaces with other training initiatives to ensure alignment and efficiency of effort.

5. **Expands Employee Perspectives—13 percent**

   Oversees continual expansion of employee perspectives about their jobs, departments, and the organization with personal participation/

incentive-driven opportunities. This function is related to but different from cross-training.

6. **Changes Behavior—13 percent**

   Leads and tracks changes in both traditional and new measures of employee transformation, contribution, and potential, including:
   - Traditional: turnover, absenteeism, negativity, healthcare costs
   - Employee and management participation in shared learning, cross-training, and mentoring
   - Active skill application of shared-learning topics
   - Development of progressive opportunity paths for employees
   - Evolution of Workforce Vitalization index for individuals and organizational entities
   - Development and use of progressive incentives, meaningful rewards, and meaningful complimentary benefits.

7. **Lead Achievement for Attaining the National Vitality Award— 9 percent**

   Provides leadership to gain the National Vitality Award for the organization.

CHAPTER 19
SUMMARY

THE MAGNITUDE OF THE EMPLOYEE STAGNATION PROBLEM is immeasurable. Stagnation threatens to destroy major corporations and organizations by crippling their competitive ability such that organizations shrivel and die at an accelerating rate. We are seeing it more and more every day.

Vitalize Your Workforce provides a practical, achievable, sustainable framework for transforming your organization from business-as-usual to a Vitality Leadership organization. The scale of the required change is so great for most organizations, coupled with the increasing pressure of market acceleration, that a new executive position is called for—a powerful leader, strongly empowered, closely aligned with the CEO, and leading and driving the fundamental changes at all levels of the organization. Consistent, focused leadership is required to assure systematic evolution for a new competitive edge.

This position is the Chief Vitality Officer, a strong and empathetic leader with an intuitive feel for the business' essence and the dynamics of stagnation and vitalization. This leader has the ability to take charge and bring about the changes necessary throughout the enterprise to accomplish the drastic fundamental changes in management style and operational culture called for to respond effectively to the problem.

NOTES

Actions: _____

_____

_____

_____

_____

Call Whom: _____

_____

_____

_____

_____

By When: _____

_____

_____

_____

_____

> "The heart of strategy is 'the essence of why the organization exists and how it thrives'."
>
> – JAMES ROBERTSON

CHAPTER 20

DISCOVERING THE STRATEGIC ESSENCE OF YOUR ORGANIZATION

By Dr. James A. Robertson

A CRITICAL COMPONENT OF VITALIZING YOUR ORGANIZATION is alignment of any improvement initiative with the organization's Strategic Essence. This alignment enables the organization and the initiative to flow together smoothly, avoiding many of the pitfalls of discord and resulting stagnation.

1. **What Is Strategic Essence?**[45]

    Professor Malcolm McDonald defines strategy as "the right things viewed from the perspective of the customer."[46] Dr. Michel Robert says that every organization has a single strategic driving force that never changes. Professor Michael Porter says the heart of strategy is differentiation.

    Combining all these thoughts and principles, it becomes apparent that the heart of strategy is "the essence of why the organization exists and how it thrives."[47] It is the purpose, the clarifier, and the differentiator.

    As such, it is absolutely critical that any Vitalize project understands and aligns with an organization's Strategic Essence. This

alignment clarifies the initiative's intention, determines the degree of flexibility of thinking for the initiative, and unifies all effort toward an important common goal.

2. **Why Is Strategic Essence Thinking Vital?**

When an organization's Strategic Essence is forgotten or ignored, clarity of communication and intention of action can become muddled and the path forward unclear. The company loses its way; it becomes stagnant.

Consider the failed Daimler Chrysler merger. The fundamental strategic driver, the essence, of Daimler Benz (Mercedes Benz) is "quality German Engineering." The driver for Chrysler is "technology innovation."[48] These drivers were fundamentally in opposition to one another, hence the failed merger. One was entrenched in "the way we have always engineered," and one was dedicated to "creating a better design." If a clear understanding existed of each business' essence, the executives could either recognize that the merger was doomed to fail, *or* they could develop initiatives to harmonize and align their individual drivers in ways that respected their differences and celebrated their combined strengths.

3. **Lack of Strategic Essence Causes Stagnation**

Ignoring Strategic Essence can cause conflict, resentment, and stagnation. An organization's essence is designed and defined by the founder, the person, or team responsible for its inception and growth.

In mature organizations, an organization's intended essence is handed over from management team to management team. When the founders leave and new management arrives, the strategic essence is often not introduced as a critical strategic component of the organization, or is not respected by the incoming leaders. When this happens, new plans and directions are often misaligned with the organization's strategic essence. Conflict in thinking among management and employees ensues, creating frustration and alienating people lower down in the organization who still respect and uphold the originating essence. Resentment and frustration develop and the employees rapidly become stagnant and demotivated.

In new organizations, tactical strategies often demand the greatest attention. If the Strategic Essence, the organization's "why," is not clear or reinforced, the fast action of various departments and their communication can bump into one another. Every group or function believes it is right, so the cause of the dysfunction becomes painfully elusive. Continual, unresolved dysfunction causes resentment, activity and interest slow down, and stagnancy begins to set in.

4. **Discovering Strategic Essence**

Discovering Strategic Essence is not fundamentally difficult. In its simplest form, the approach is to interview each member of the executive team one-on-one for an hour and ask "What is the essence of the organization and how does it thrive?" followed by several other key questions. Generally, executives will think deeply, often indicating it is the first time they have been asked this question. After a while, they offer a statement that is fairly close to what they feel is the truth. If the answers are familiar and similar across executives, the current belief of the organization's Strategic Essence can be easily defined, and with facilitated dialogue, refined into a clear communicable statement.

When the organization is mature, and a number of executives are newly hired from the outside, the results may be very different. In these organizations, it may be necessary to interview a much greater number of people, including mid-level managers who have been with the organization for a long time, to understand the originating Strategic Essence.

The value of these interviews is to determine the gap. The gap between the new executive's view of the organization's Strategic Essence, which may include what is considered necessary to compete in the market today, and the traditional employees' view of the organization's Strategic Essence may be wide. Misaligned intentions can easily cause discord, miscommunication, and resentment. Any gap requires facilitation of dialogue to clarify the Strategic Essence of the company today and to align the new executive with the thinking and actions of their valuable employees.

If this inquiry highlights considerable disparity in the responses, further initiatives are required to drill down and manage the conversation across all key executives until the true essence, the purpose for the company, is firmly established.

In a situation where there have been many mergers and acquisitions, additional work may be required to harmonize the Strategic

Essence across all business units/organizational entities to arrive at a definition for the entire enterprise.

5. **The Benefits of Strategic Essence Thinking**

   Fundamentally, Strategic Essence thinking helps to smooth the way for an intentional, focused Vitality improvement initiative. The benefits of Strategic Essence include:

   - Establishing a clear, unifying definition of what *really* drives the organization.
   - Creating a common vocabulary and thought process regarding the requirements for the organization to thrive.
   - Defining a filter for determining what to do, and what not to do, to ensure the company's success.
   - Creating a diagnostic aid to identify operations that are out of alignment or not operating at their optimum, and situations causing stagnation.
   - Clarifying initiatives required to Vitalize the organization.

6. **An Example of How Ignoring Strategic Essence Crippled a Project**

   Following is an example of how ignoring Strategic Essence crippled a Business Information System implementation project:

CASE STUDY

FREIGHT CLEARING AGENT[49]

A consultant was called into a freight forwarding and clearing business to troubleshoot a project that had been stalled for twelve months. During a one-hour, one-on-one interview with each member of the executive team, the consultant asked, "What is the essence of the business and how does it thrive?" From the responses, he ascertained that the core of the business was a service promise: *"If we promise you delivery by a certain date and time, but the shipment is delayed, we will make good your loss."* The key factor was that this client organization concentrated its business on the 10 percent of the market where time was of the essence when it came to clearing shipments. It was very good at serving this market and was a market leader in terms of service levels. It had very loyal customers and very loyal staff who were committed to this service promise.

The consultant then interviewed the owner of the software company supplying the new software and facilitating the system implementation. This individual made it clear his focus was not on meeting the needs of expedient shipments, but on the 90 percent of clearing and forwarding activities where the time required to clear a shipment was *not* of the essence. As a consequence, he was not particularly concerned with the service levels required for expedient shipments.

When the consultant reported this finding to the executive who had initiated the engagement, the executive immediately responded, "*Of course! That's it!*" That single discovery fully explained the tensions, frustration, and lack of commitment to service of the entire "sorry saga" for a project that had run for eighteen months and caused nothing but heartache and frustration.

The project was immediately terminated and the contract awarded to a service provider who intuitively understood the service promise to the client. Its software went in without difficulty.

7. The Role of Strategic Essence in Vitalizing Your Workforce

What role does Strategic Essence thinking play in Vitalizing your workforce?

The Strategic Essence is a key element, the starting point to focus the attention of both the client and consultant teams on what is truly important to the organization. This focus increases overall project effectiveness and efficiency, significantly helps to contain costs, and reduces risk. These critical factors result in an overall project outcome that is dramatically better than would be achieved without this component.

Vitalize Your Workforce strongly advocates Strategic Essence thinking in every organization improvement project, whether a Vitalize project, an ERP implementation, or any other significant initiative to enhance organization effectiveness and efficiency.

CHAPTER 20
SUMMARY

STRATEGIC ESSENCE IS THAT FUNDAMENTAL SET OF ATTRIbutes responsible for an organization's existence that provides a continuity of purpose and focus across your organization.

All of the organization's activities are impacted by the clarity and forthright communication of its Strategic Essence. Lack of clarity and lack of clear consistent communication can critically compromise and cripple an organization, causing resentment and discord. On the other hand, when initiatives are aligned with and support the Strategic Essence, the effectiveness of employees and the efficiency of all operations are dramatically improved.

Determining the organization's Strategic Essence is a fundamental building block in the process of Vitalizing Your Workforce, optimizing your leadership, and enhancing the power of your Vision, Mission, Culture, and Policies, which will look at in the following chapters.

NOTES

Actions: _____

_____

_____

_____

_____

Call Whom: _____

_____

_____

_____

_____

By When: _____

_____

_____

_____

_____

"The real voyage of discovery consists not in seeking new lands but seeing with new eyes."

– MARCEL PROUST

CHAPTER 21

VITALIZING YOUR VISION

Vision Is a Common Business Concept—or Is It?

YOUR VISION STATEMENT IS YOUR KEY LEADERSHIP DOCument. According to Business Dictionary, a Vision statement is "an inspirational description of what a company or organization would like to achieve or accomplish in the mid-term or long-term future." A Vision statement serves as the North Star or compass for your organization. It provides the organization's reason for being, what it wants to accomplish, and what it wants to be known for in the future." The Vision sets the overall direction to be shared and accomplished by all employees, suppliers, and affiliates.

You know all of this, so what else is new?
Everything.

As related many times in this book, the world and market are changing fast. Technology is accelerating so fast that obsolescence is becoming the norm. The influx and character of Generations X, Y, and Z with their technology, social media, networking, and instantaneous research competencies is so contrary to slow, traditional control-oriented organizations that each group hardly recognizes the other. Add to that the complexities of world chaos that are getting closer daily, and hardly anything is familiar anymore.

When was the last time you read your company's Vision statement? Does your Vision communicate with your customers, employees, and suppliers—that you know it is a new day? That you know it is no longer business as usual; that you need to lead in a different way? Does it openly recognize the need to develop and leverage the potential of all your employees as a competitive edge—and not just your top talent?

Leaders today must be present, current, real, and resilient. Leaders need to be more visible and relatable, understanding that each success and function requires all of your employees' interest and energy. Each employee needs to hear directly from you and buy-in to the belief that his or her presence and work in your company is valuable—that he or she is a recognized part of a company ready to take on new challenges.

Why revisit your Vision statement now? Sadly, Vision statements are often written but are:

- inaccurate or inappropriate
- taken for granted or forgotten
- outdated
- poorly communicated across an organization's various levels and functions
- communicated only once a year with little reinforcement
- missing the important declaration of intention to become a progressive thinking, learning organization that thrives on the Vitality and potential of its employees

Any one or combination of these factors renders the Vision statement ineffective. An ineffective Vision increases employee malaise. Furthermore, once a Vision statement is written, many leaders move on assuming employees hear and care about the Vision. In reality, the majority of employees may not even know there *is* a Vision for the company, let alone understand and relate to it. In essence, they are mentally and emotionally unattached. To make things worse, this disconnect is huge and most of the time remains unnoticed.

"We are not in a business-as-usual time, and your employees know it."

Create a New North Star—with Clear Intention

The real North Star today includes your declared intention to transform your business into a progressive thinking, learning organization that has Vitality, proactive interest, and participation at all levels and in all functions. It openly recognizes the need to develop employee skills and activate their potential for greater communication, collaboration, problem solving, idea generation, and resilience.

A leadership Vision statement today must clearly state: "We are moving beyond business as usual, permanently." Add examples that demonstrate your understanding of the need for "quick responsiveness to change and opportunity, fast issue resolution and problem solving, and ongoing evolution of skills and opportunities for all."

> *"Employees today need to connect with what is in it for them."*

If your Vision statement expresses a goal for only one aspect of the business, such as: "Our goal is to become a billion-dollar company," you are missing the mark.

Some companies combine multiple aspects of business goals into the Vision statement, such as:

- "To become a billion-dollar company…" (quantitative statement)
- "To become the leader in…" (qualitative statement)
- "To beat X company in…" (competitive declaration)
- "To be like…" (role model statements)

They are also missing the mark. These Visions provide more specific goals and ways to measure success, but they have little or no direct connection to your employees. Few employees today will make the leap of faith to embrace a Vision that does not relate to them as well as to your market.

Start by Listening

Talk with employees on every level and in every function of your organization. Learn first-hand how many employees know there is a Vision for the company, where they can find it, and in general what it says. Ask them whether they care. If they don't care, either they don't know you have one, or they haven't thought about your Vision statement for a long time. Either way, they are disconnected. If they do care, it's likely they think it is important for the company to know where it is going, but they don't think it applies to them. Again, either way you are in trouble. How do you lead your employees if they don't connect with where you want to go?

Then Expand by Talking

Next, lead open, non-judgmental discussion at the Leadership Team level about the evolving role of your Vision statement in general. Then examine the effectiveness of your current Vision statement. Some questions you might ask are:

- Who is the *real* audience for the Vision statement? Who else needs to know the Vision? Why? Who is the priority? Does your current Vision speak to that priority?
- Is your priority your board and your investors? That's fine, but not enough. Who is your next priority? What priority are your employees—the people who make your company work?
- What do they need to know?
- Does your Vision statement include the clear intention to become a progressive thinking, learning organization? Does it emphasize respect and the Vitalization of employee potential everywhere in the organization?
- Does your Vision need to be communicated differently for different locations, levels, and functions within the organization?
- How is your Vision statement communicated now? Does a one-size-fits-all approach work?
- Where and how often do you share the Vision for your company? Once a year?
- How easy is it for employees to see your Vision? Where can they find it?

Create a Vision That Includes "What's in It for Me?"

All employees need your leadership. They need to see it, hear it, and feel it. Vitalize your Vision statement annually. Take your time. Answering "What's in it for me?" doesn't have to be a promise. A Vision is an intention. In addition to stating where the company is going and what it stands for, vitalize your workforce by stating that you have a Vision for your employees too. Emphasize your commitment to expanding employee skills and application of those skills—expanding employee potential as you expand the business. Be clear. Let them know that a new future for you also means a new future and new opportunities for them.

Appoint a Chief Vitality Officer

Create a post for a Chief Vitality Officer reporting to the CEO. Fill that post with an expert who can lead development and implementation of innovative projects to motivate and empower employees. Add responsibility for effectively communicating your new Vision to the entire organization in a way employees in all functions can hear it. Add transformation of your management teams from managing numbers to proven excellence in people-leadership as criteria for hire and promotion to people-leadership positions.

Repeat, Repeat, and Repeat

Repeat your Vision statement often. Instilling any idea in the midst of all the communication interference today is a challenge. Repeat the essence of your Vision in many ways, in whole or in part. Add it to your intranet newsletter; add it as an opening visual to presentations; add it to posters placed around the organization; add it to podcasts by you and a variety of your leaders. Stay with it. You are becoming a visible, consistent, and recognized as a market leader of a Vitalized company.

The key?

Once you set the stage by declaring your intention to become a progressive thinking, learning organization, implement company-wide programs designed to expand employee perspective and capability. Without this declaration, you are still communicating from the remote business-as-usual mindset, and that is the response you will receive.

CHAPTER 21
SUMMARY

TODAY'S EMPLOYEES NEED TO UNDERSTAND HOW YOUR Vision for your company affects their daily work, their career, and their personal lives. An ineffective Vision statement increases employee disconnect and stagnation.

Announce your intention to become a progressive thinking, learning organization that is full of Vitality, one focused on expanding the potential of your greatest asset—your employees. Then cascade that Vision across your organization at all levels in ways your employees can best understand it.

NOTES

Actions: _____

_____

_____

_____

_____

_____

Call Whom: _____

_____

_____

_____

_____

By When: _____

_____

_____

_____

_____

> *"It goes without saying that no company, small or large, can win over the long run without energized employees who believe in the mission and understand how to achieve it."*
>
> – JACK WELCH

CHAPTER 22

MAGNIFYING YOUR MISSION

YOUR MISSION STATEMENT CONVERTS YOUR VISION STATEment into how you intend to achieve your vision. It provides a deeper level of clarity for your employees, suppliers, affiliates, and investors. It is the foundation for a collaborative sense of purpose for your organization.

Traditional elements of a Mission statement include:

- What we do: "We develop the best product and/or service to…."
- Who do we do it for: "Our primary customer is…."
- How we plan to reach our goals: "By creating excellence in manufacturing" or "By purchasing and integrating leading-edge technology or research."
- Our value differentiator: "Being the best in customer service" or "Providing the most advanced technology or medical care."

A well-conceived Mission statement also includes your core values as an organization and the behaviors you expect from all employees with each other and in all transactions.

These qualities might include:

- Respect for all employees, races, religions, creeds
- Honesty and trust

- Teamwork and proactive problem-solving
- Support for individuals, compassion for their family responsibilities

These are important human values. They define the qualities you are going to uphold as you achieve your Mission, what qualities you expect and respect for your corporate Culture, and what qualities you will uphold in your corporate Policies.

Who Knows Your Mission?

Take time to talk with employees on different levels and in different functions about your company Mission. It is likely that the executive levels will know your company Mission because they have to perform to achieve it. Your Mission is their touchstone to measure their personal success.

Aside from your Executive Team, how many employees in your organization are really connected to what you are trying to do? How many employees can articulate your Mission, your overall strategy for reaching your Vision? Do you know?

What if all they really know is "We are a leader in high performing cars," or "We are leaders in medicated Band-Aids?" If you ask them to finish the sentence "Our Mission is to become ____ by doing ____" can they fill in the blanks? If they don't know, how can they have a personal connection to your business? How do they know where to focus their efforts? Or is business-as-usual okay with you?

Magnifying Your Mission

Simon Sinek says it clearly: "Start with Why?"[50] Why is the company here? Why do you have employees? What do you want them to do? What mountain do you want them to climb? Do they know?

Do they know that it is a new day? That you are clear on your new Mission to become a Vitalized organization, committed to developing and expanding your employee potential as the new competitive edge? Do you state that you want your employees to come along with you to achieve this competitive edge?

How prominent is your Mission in the minds and hearts of your employees, the employees who need to know the most so they can help you get here?

CASE STUDY

PUBLIX SUPERMARKET[51]

Publix is one of *Fortune*'s 100 Best companies to work for (1998-2016). Among Publix's many outstanding awards, Temkin Customer Experience Ratings ranks it at #1 for Customer Experience, #2 for Customer Service, and #3 for Customer Loyalty. Something significant is going on here.

> *"Our mission at Publix is to be the premier quality food retailer in the world."*

How did Publix reach that ranking? First, it declared, "Our mission at Publix is to be the premier quality food retailer in the world." It then identified the areas that would lead it to the #1 ranking. It said it would be:

- Passionately focused on customer value
- Intolerant of waste
- Dedicated to the dignity, value and employment security of our associates
- Devoted to the highest standards of stewardship for our stockholders, and
- Involved as responsible citizens in our communities.

For the full reference, see www.publix.com. Go to "About Us," then "Company Overview." You can also find its employee ratings on several social media sites: Facebook, Twitter, Snapchat, Instagram.

Was Publix successful in meeting its goals? Do its employees feel respected?

After defining its Mission to be the premier quality food retailer in the world, it enrolled its employees in identifying large and small actions that would contribute to achieving this goal. Employees helped craft their own department's Contributing Mission Statement to support the company goals. They identified what actions to take, as well as where and how. They set up accountability records. They also made recommendations for how to strengthen each other's work so the customer experiences quality all the time. They set up recognition milestones for individuals and teams, including how they can celebrate achievements together.

This is working with a collaborative sense of purpose at its best.

To Magnify Your Mission, Start Wherever You Are

Look at your current Mission statement. What does it really say? Ask your Leadership Team, your middle managers, and your employees in every department and function. What do they think it says?

Some employees might have great awareness of your Mission statement, and some might not even know what a Mission statement is, or that you even have one. This is all good information. It is important for you to understand your employees' level of awareness so you know where to start.

Employee inquiry can be led by a designated in-house team, or you can engage outside experts to conduct one-on-one and group interviews for you. Either way, it is important for you to learn:

- How many employees know of your company's Mission statement
- Where they can see your company's Mission statement
- How it is currently communicated
- Whether different functions within the company require different forms of communication
- How many employees can convey the concepts within your Mission statement
- Whether the Mission statement clearly states becoming a progressive thinking, learning organization
- Whether it commits to becoming a Vitalized organization
- What employees need to do differently to support your new Mission

Once you acquire this knowledge, you have enough practical information to add Vitality to your Mission statement. Ask new questions and strive to understand the employees' answers. The employee alignment and commitment you receive for your Mission is up to you.

Stimulating Corporate Vitality Starts at the Top

Employees need to hear, see, and feel that leadership is fully involved in creating a future for the organization and that you are increasing your Vitality to achieve it. Assure your Mission statement is:

1. **Current:** Relevant to today's market, today's products, and today's challenges. Market dynamics are moving fast. Schedule regular reviews

with your employee groups to ensure its real-time practicality in a changing world.

2. **Clear:** Written in a language that connects with employees on all levels and all functions of the organization; and a language that connects with customers, suppliers, affiliates, and investors. It needs to be succinct, action-oriented, results achievable, and measurable.

3. **Prominent:** Consistently visible in more than one place. Every employee needs to know the organization has focus, Vitality, and fortitude if he or she is going to dance effectively with change.

4. **Communicated well:** Provided with enough repetition to produce awareness and easy recall. Increase how often you repeat your Mission statement and where it appears—aloud in meetings, in planning documents, newsletters, your intranet, at employee events, and posters placed in high traffic areas.

Cascade your Mission statement to all levels and departments of the organization in a way that the employees in each department will understand it. The daily language of marketing is different from the daily language of manufacturing. Enlist your people-leaders in each department to assist in ensuring clear communication and understanding.

"Enlist the help of a good communicator from each department."

Mentor these people-leaders to carry your message to their departments so each sector of employees understands its personal connection, value, and contribution to the organization as a whole. Help your employees to remember why they work for your company, and why they are excited and proud to do so.

When employees have an *aha moment* about where they fit and how they contribute, interest and commitment rise, and Vitality and loyalty soar.

Evolving Your Organization

Many companies are already progressive thinking and learning organizations with leading-edge strategic planning and new concept development. Some of the most visible companies known for being progressive are Google, Zappos, Facebook, and Apple. Their Mission statements keep this positioning and these key capabilities at the forefront of their employees' minds.

Commit to freeing your employees from tradition-imposed stagnation. Create a Mission statement that leads your employees to becoming excellent in spontaneous problem-solving anytime, anywhere. This critical skill builds greater collaboration and generates more understanding and more opportunities. This is Vitality!

Your transformation to a progressive thinking, learning organization with high Vitality requires overt leadership commitment, communication, action, and consistency. This message must be visible for everyone as a permanent goal. Support this goal with a commitment to implement new programs to Vitalize Your Workforce and your company as a whole.

Is There Urgency? It's Your Choice.

Organizations function on human energy, wisdom, time, and commitment—from the least noticed jobs to the most visible. Chaotic situations affect everyone. In the past, it was easier for organizations to minimize surprises and maintain a smooth workflow. Today, the definition of status quo is changing daily. The economy fluctuates, sometimes greatly. Terrorism is front-page news every day, instilling fear and disrupting confidence. External and internal demands require an ever-increasing ability to respond effectively, quickly.

What are we learning from this? Referencing *Team of Teams* by Ret. General Stanley McChrystal, "the smartest response for those in charge is to give small groups the freedom to experiment, sharing what they learn across the entire organization."

For commercial organizations, this means developing capabilities for faster planning, quicker action, and instant response in all phases of the business. This goal must become part of your Mission statement. This means leadership must consistently build collaborative problem solving, open communication, and the ability for spontaneous teamwork across your entire workforce.

This is an inside job. Simply stating your intention to become a progressive thinking, learning organization that is Vitalized doesn't mean your workforce will understand it or believe it, let alone do it. Building trust with visible action steps systematically expands your employees' perspective and confidence about the organization. The faster they experience your dedication to leading for greater vitality and sustainability, the faster they will transition to join you.

CHAPTER 22
SUMMARY

YOUR MISSION STATEMENT CONVERTS YOUR VISION INTO concrete, specific, and actionable steps. Update your Mission to state a clear commitment to becoming a progressive thinking, learning organization that has vibrant, flexible employees ready to respond to new challenges and new opportunities anywhere, any time. This commitment sets the tone and the strength to say it is a new day and that you are leading in a new way.

Cascade your Mission statement to all employees in the organization. Enlist your people-leaders to communicate your Mission effectively in a way that each function or group needs to hear. Help employees align their jobs and their personal visions to your Mission. Build momentum with Vitality!

NOTES

Actions: _____

_____

_____

_____

_____

Call Whom: _____

_____

_____

_____

_____

_____

By When: _____

_____

_____

_____

_____

> *"To win in the marketplace you must first win in the workplace. Employee engagement is the key to activating a high performing workforce."*
>
> – FORMER CAMPBELL'S SOUP CEO, DOUG CONANT

CHAPTER 23

KICK-STARTING YOUR CULTURE

CULTURE REFERS TO THE INTERNAL AND EXTERNAL WORKING environments of an organization: its beliefs, standards of communication, and desired behavior for everyone involved. Vitalizing your Culture requires clearly written guidelines for a strong, positive-thinking, productive environment that helps create a workplace where people trust the company to support them in offering their best. These guidelines include but are not limited to:

Together, these cultural guidelines create a visible, value-based brand of leadership recognized inside and outside the organization.

- Clear communication
- Reward for quality work Timely issue resolution
- Respect
- Supportive leadership
- Teamwork
- Timely issue resolution
- Honesty
- Collaborative problem-solving

Johnson & Johnson is a good example:

Johnson & Johnson is an exemplary leader in defining a high-quality corporate Culture with clear, written guidelines for behavior and results. The company states its Vision, Mission, and Cultural guidelines in a carefully crafted, well-documented, and visible Credo (a written definition of the company's philosophy for doing business).

Its Credo speaks directly to the company's six primary areas of interest: employees, customers, suppliers, investors, family, and communities (worldwide). Within these six, the company recognizes areas of importance for a quality business and work environment.

For example, in the employee arena, Johnson & Johnson expresses respect and dignity for every individual; recognizes great work habits and ethics; strives to provide a strong sense of job security; provides fair and adequate compensation; and provides a safe working environment for employees. The company also encourages the freedom to offer suggestions and complaints, and provides equal opportunity for development and advancement.

All organizations need this level of thought and preparation when defining their corporate Culture.

This Sounds Good. So, What is the Problem?

Global research statistics concur that over 85 percent of the workforce is disengaged; employees are stagnant. If a high percentage of employees are personally stagnant, then there is a culture problem. If 90 percent don't like their jobs and 65 percent want to leave the organization when their work goes unrecognized,[52] then there is a Culture problem.

This is a critical awareness, as stagnant employees beget more stagnant employees, and further Culture problems. Stagnant employees spend more time in worry, stress, and pain. The less they see and hear from their Leadership, the more insecure and remote they become with their confidence disintegrating daily.

Declining personal security leads to decreased communication and relationships between diverse cultural or generational groups. Employees with a tendency to be loud and critical become more vocal, and quiet contributors grow more reticent and less involved. "What's in it for me?" becomes more pervasive all the time until "There is nothing in it for me" prevails and stagnation has reached its nadir.

It is Time to Focus on Vitality!

When employees work in and share a stated corporate Culture that recognizes, encourages, and reinforces the high value contribution and potential of each individual, confidence grows. Employees are then more confident in sharing ideas and collaborating to solve problems. They are open to learning new skills and helping the organization be in the world in a new way.

This vibrancy requires a strong, clear progressive thinking, learning Culture dedicated to the Vitality of all employees—a Culture with a positive, communicating ethos that believes individual strengths are expandable gifts to be shared, respected, developed at any age, and in any function. This is the hallmark of a Culture that believes in offering skill development that increases employee value and contribution at work, at home, and in their communities.

"Vitality is the opposite of stagnation."

Where Does a Company Start?

Recognize that stagnation is rife and that a dramatic turnaround is required. Actively choose to Vitalize your workforce. Resolving the causes of employee stagnation might not be in your sights right now or be a focus in your current strategic plan, but please understand, the world won't wait. You need to care and take action.

Everything is in a state of flux. Countries are building new islands. Groups are disbanding, morphing, and reassembling miles away overnight. Accelerating technology is changing what people can do and how they can think, daily. Employees in your care know about these changes. They feel them, and they are increasingly aware that as employees, they may be standing still.

Progressive thinking, learning organizations recognize the imperative to vitalize their workforce. These organizations establish foundational programs across their organizations to expand employee perspectives, skills, and potential for their work and their lives.

*"Enhancing individual potential
raises employee interest and confidence."*

Expanding and enhancing individual potential raises employee interest and confidence. Confidence, in turn, expands interest, the willingness to learn new skills, and the eagerness for mentoring. It creates open minds to try new things. Increased confidence increases communication and willing collaboration. It increases interest in meeting new people and groups and opens employees to accepting continually emerging opportunities—one small step at time. Above all, it raises employee security because employees believe that they are better able to support their families and contribute to their communities in a greater way. This is Vitality!

"Organizations with Vitality will win."

What does Vitality Mean for Your Organization?

Compare where you are now to where you want or need to be. Is "sufficient" good enough for you, or is "extraordinary" what you need? What is extraordinary? Choose where you want to be and go for it!

Webster's definition of "Vitality" is: strength, verve, vigor, dynamism, energy, vivacity. It stems from the Latin root that means "vital life force."

The more Vitality you have in all of its forms, the stronger and more purposeful you are, the more you learn, and the more you want to apply who you are for the betterment of the greater good.

In my review of over 2,400 employees across all levels of responsibility, from over twenty industries, I found that most of those employees had limited perspectives about their companies and limited perspectives about their own opportunities. Not only were they unaware of their companies' Vision and Mission statements, but very few knew the scope and depth of their companies' offerings. When asked about their work, most had little or no understanding of the functions adjacent to their own jobs, e.g., what department or function produced their incoming work or where it went after leaving them.

This means they really didn't know where their jobs fit into the bigger picture or the importance of their work. They knew little about how their responsibilities tied in with other functions. They could only guess about the content, purpose, and timing of information flows between departments. And when there were issues, few know how to solve them. How would you define this Culture?

The best responses in our inquiry came from those in fields that required fast decisions and immediate backup from their team members to be successful. These included: fast-food workers, medical caregivers, first responders, law enforcement, and safety workers. In these professions, the team feels an instant impact when someone is absent. For them, immediate need drives their Culture and their collaboration.

The larger the organization, the less perspective employees had for where they fit in and the more their perspectives centered on the day-to-day repetition of what was on their desks. These employees had resigned themselves to their jobs long ago. Rarely did they take the initiative to learn about their adjacent functions or get to know the people in those departments.

What Is Missing?

Many participants said their companies did not have Cultures that encouraged or rewarded open-minded inquiry. They had no mandate to learn, nor any process for understanding other departments, no permission, and no personal benefit for taking the initiative.

> *"Lack of encouragement, permission, and process = stagnation."*

These employees felt they had to stay quietly in their place, reluctant to explore. They worked with little or no connection to the rest of the organization, and with little dialogue about how to improve the work coming in or going out. Many of these employees had worked in the same position for years. Some liked the consistency. However, many of them felt forgotten and undervalued. They knew they could do more, but they had no idea whether their untapped skills and interests could be useful in other departments, and no idea how to find out. They were stuck, demotivated, and disengaged. They were stagnant.

> *"Stagnant employees see their jobs as paid jails."*

Ignored and unrecognized, stagnant employees feel their capabilities and potential are wasted. They know it, and many resent it.

CASE STUDY

CAMPBELL'S SOUP[53]

Campbell's Soup was a 2010 Catalyst Winner. In 2005, Campbell's sales were stagnant. It had the lowest Gallup engagement scores for any Fortune 500 company. Campbell's decided to make a change. It immediately started a comprehensive initiative called *Winning in the Workplace, Winning in the Marketplace, Winning with Women*. Campbell's went all out in its campaign to increase the Vitality in all employee groups and develop a proactive Culture of diversity and inclusion. Within three years, it transformed its company Culture, winning Gallup's "Great Workplace Award" in 2008 and 2009.

Campbell's began with a robust inclusion strategy that crossed department lines and brought together the workforce from all manufacturing plant sites as well. It developed a company-wide Culture of mentoring through affinity networks across the company.

Its Women of Campbell's Network became the flagship group. Then it developed the Campbell's BRIDGE Network to act as a bridge across the various generations represented within the workforce.

Its OPEN Network celebrated LGBTQ families by asking for family photos and videos that were then displayed near various workplace entrances. These photos became the topic of discussion for a panel of senior women. All of these activities served to bring the workforce together in respect and appreciation as a cohesive whole.

Along with these changes, Campbell's included accountability in its review package for compensation considerations. Active, engaged employees received rewards.

With this Culture shift, Campbell's Soup went from the bottom of the Fortune 500 listing to better than average in productivity and returns. It is a prime example of company Culture affecting its bottom line.

Getting Real—What Is the Impact?

Personal stagnation and lack of employee engagement is expensive and debilitating. Negativity and healthcare costs rise. Absenteeism and turnover increase, and loyalty declines. With consistent action to vitalize employees, the results change dramatically:

- Companies with engaged workers have a greater than 6 percent higher net profit[54]
- Engaged companies have five times higher shareholder returns over five years[55]

The increased ROI of engagement comes from the Engagement-Profit Chain.[56] Vitalized employees lead to:

- Higher service, quality, and productivity, which leads to…
- Higher customer satisfaction, which leads to…
- Increased sales (repeat business and referrals), which leads to…
- Higher levels of profit, which leads to…
- Higher shareholder returns (i.e., stock price)

What Is the Message?

"To win in the marketplace you must first win in the workplace. Employee engagement is the key to activating a high performing workforce."

– FORMER CAMPBELL'S SOUP CEO, DOUG CONANT

Take action. Establish commitment to develop your organizational Culture to become a progressive thinking, learning organization. Lead with clear focus on building corporate Vitality in your Vision, Mission, and Culture. These key leadership documents set the "what, where, when, why, and how" of your business.

Add to your communication that it is a new day, with ever-new leadership focus, action, and involvement to magnify the Vitality of your organization. Institute the Chief Vitality Officer position and function. Differentiate the accountabilities between Human Resources and Vitality Leadership so your employees know it really is a new day.

CASE STUDY

LAWRENCE[57]

Sipping coffee from a Styrofoam cup, Lawrence sat halfway back in his stiff chair calmly watching Barbara, the HR Director, shuffle papers at her standing desk across from him. She wore the usual corporate ensemble: dark blazer and silk top, frosted hair twisted up in a claw clip. She moved in an unhurried way, but she covered a lot of territory.

Lawrence glanced through the window at the parking lot outside and fought the urge to adjust his tie. As his final interview wound down, he still had no real sense of his future at Pacific Mechanical. He wanted this job. The moment he had stepped into the building, something about the place had felt right to him.

Although he sat in the company's expansive central office, which was bustling with activity, the space had the same warm feel as the local deli around the corner from where he lived. Mort and his wife, Marilyn, had owned the deli for thirty years. At Mort's, every customer received a greeting by name, often including the names of family members as well: "I hope Margaret's feeling better today, Joe."

Pacific Mechanical felt like the same kind of place.

Barbara opened a fresh folder, paused, then asked, "Lawrence, I have two final questions for you. First, what does the term *family* mean to you? And then I would like you to tell me what your life will look like five years from this day."

Taken off guard by the intimacy of the questions, Lawrence's personal shield came up. He cleared his throat. "You mean my own family? Err, can I answer the second question first?"

Looking over her half-moon reading glasses, Barbara nodded and focused on him. Lawrence had never plumbed a sink or installed sheet metal, the company's core activities. His BA in history offered no preparation for the daily activities of engineering, contracting, or project management. As a server at Scorbies Restaurant, Lawrence had impressed Pacific Mechanical's company president, Don Milbrand; and the next day, to Lawrence's surprise, Barbara called to set up their first interview.

Don seemed to select his talent at random. His method went against all the science of Human Resource Management, but after nineteen years of working with Don, Barbara easily created custom jobs for unusual people. Nearly all of the apparently random candidates became key, successful contributors to the large but careful growth of the company.

Lawrence slid farther back into his chair. His voice sounded firm. "I want to work in a company that is based on respect and dignity. I have a reasonable level of confidence, but I'm also well aware that I have a lot to learn. Five years from today, I expect to have learned a lot more than I can even imagine now. My job at Scorbies keeps me on my toes with creative problem solving, and the money is really good. But five years from now, I'd like to drive around town and see projects that I worked on, buildings that I helped make happen."

Barbara smiled. The unwritten slogan of the company was, "We build awesome jobs!" an approach that mirrored the Milbrand family's values. There was a light tap on her office door and Don's bald head appeared. Without speaking, he held up a half-full coffeepot.

"More coffee, Lawrence?" he asked.

Lawrence tried to stand in respect for the CEO of a $700 million company, but his notepad slid off onto the floor, spilling out his resume and several forms.

"No, no sit down," Don said, refilling Lawrence's cup. "I pour coffee for everyone around here. It's one of the things I do well." Ron smiled and headed for the door. He turned back to ask, "Has she talked to you about the family yet?"

"Just getting there, Don. Would you like to do the honors?" Barbara asked.

"This might be rusty, but here is the deal." He placed the coffeepot on a handy shelf.

"We all have families of some sort, right?"

Fearful that he would have to describe his own semi-dysfunctional living situation, Lawrence nodded.

"We take great pains and expense to make sure the Pacific family is the most effective and functional family you know. We are all different. We are not always right. We get short with each other. There is plenty of pressure and plenty of challenges to go around." He paused for a second, and his face became animated.

"We are an *effective family business*, and we like to put the emphasis equally on each word. I will assign you fifty hours of work to do next week, and forty hours to do it in. I will not micro-manage you. I expect you to ask for help when you need it and give help whenever you can.

"Our success depends on your success. You'll need a passionate approach to work and lifelong learning. I care what is happening in your life because it affects your quality of work here. You have clear access to every leader. There are no middle managers. However, your work will be ranked against all others in your division. You earn A, B, or C grades. Cs usually have their resumes out for a new job. We are all vulnerable, transparent, and accountable. We give real performance reviews and one helluva Christmas party."

Don Milbrand paused, distracted by an elderly Asian man riding an electric scooter through the parking lot. The scooter stopped as a car pulled beside him. The driver of the car got out, assisted the man into the passenger seat, and then stowed the scooter in the trunk. A moment later, they drove out of the parking lot.

Don said, "That was Swiss Nagasaki. He's a master plumber, and I was his apprentice. I used to make coffee for him every morning. Any guess how long Swiss has worked with Pacific Mechanical?"

Lawrence shook his head. The numbers didn't seem to work.

"My dad started the company in 1947. Swiss joined up in '53. He retired after fifty years, in 2003. He's been back to work nearly every week since. He just won't stop coming. We keep an office for him. We provide a driver on the days he wants to work, and we still pay him. On our toughest repair jobs, he is still one of our best resources.

"Loyalty is one of our three Core Values. Family, Loyalty, and Respect are all two-way streets for us. Did Barbara ask you the five-year question?" He glanced at her.

Lawrence nodded. "Yes, I think I answered it."

"We have three people in this office today who have more than fifty-five years with our company. We have over a dozen with more than twenty years. We are now fifty times bigger, revenue-wise, than when my dad ran it. Do you know how we did that?"

He leaned in. "With people like you, Lawrence. Only bring your very best self to work every day. That is the only thing we accept from each other. And it seems to work. I believe the harder I work, the luckier I get."

He watched the younger man's face. "So, where will you be in five years?"

"Right here, Mr. Milbrand."

"Atta boy, Lawrence. That will be only the beginning. Think of how much you will learn for us and for yourself. Morning coffee is a tradition around here. Most of the staff are here about 7:00 a.m. See you then." He picked up the coffeepot and left the office.

"Welcome to the Family," Barbara said, smiling, as she slid papers across the desk toward him. "Here are your intake forms."

Leadership Team Values

Traditional cultural considerations such as background, language, education, and work experience will always be important. The twenty-first century business, however, must include a commitment to developing and expanding Vitality throughout the organization, across all employees and functions.

Here are some simple guidelines for communicating your new commitment:

1. Provide consistent, visible communication of your new Vision, Mission, and Culture statements for all employees, suppliers, affiliates, and investors.

2. Frequently repeat your message in a variety of mediums. Change the message from the standard "This is what we stand for…" to "What is new? Why something new? Why is it important?"

3. Be clear and be real. Admit "business as usual" is long gone. Consider this message:

4. "We are all aware of what is going on in the world, but we can do more than just survive. We can thrive—together. We are ahead of the curve with our focus on Vitality and the extraordinary value and potential of our people. We have a lot to learn to become truly Vitalized, but we are clear. We have the right people, for the right time. We have the right goals and the right heart. The time is now."

5. Be visible, involved, and present. The days of remote leadership are gone. The further away employees are from the CEO in the chain of command, the less confident and more uninvolved they are. They need to know that their leadership team sees them, respects them, and feels they are important. Employees need to know their leader is at the helm guiding the ship.

6. Make communication as respectfully personal as possible. Technology is great, but be careful—avoid the temptation to retreat into habitual safe distances such as email and speaking through others.

7. Increase your emphasis on people-leadership. Often, employees will leave a job or organization to escape a manager who has no people skills or interest. Be clear about the need to build greater people-leadership skills across the organization.

8. Establish shared learning, delegation, problem solving, and mentoring as core skills required of everyone from the top down. Emphasize and mentor employees with natural people-leadership skills. Create and communicate people-leadership values and the need for people-leadership in management positions.

9. Reassign managers who are not people-leaders; they crush initiative and cause employee stagnation.

10. Cascade your target culture, beliefs, and guidelines to all employees, customers, suppliers, affiliates, and investors in a way that each level and function can understand.

"Take time to create a better way."

Share your Culture statement in the language of each department. The daily language of Shipping is not the same daily language as Program Management. Appropriate language helps the members of each department understand their connection, importance, and contribution to developing a progressive thinking, learning culture that is vibrant and successful.

Take time to help employees know the importance of their jobs. Help them know how their participation benefits the organization, their department, and, most importantly, them personally. Help them understand that greater participation creates more opportunities.

Identify the natural people-leaders in each department or function. Mentor them to join your communication team to assist in conveying what your new Culture statement means for them and their department. Let your people-leaders develop experience in asking for feedback for improvement, and working with your Chief Vitality Office team to help in continually developing a better way. Collaborating to Vitalize your workforce *is* Vitality!

CHAPTER 23
SUMMARY

CULTURE REFERS TO AN ORGANIZATION'S INTERNAL AND external working environments: its beliefs, guidelines for respectful interactions, level of responsibility for individual and team behavior, quality of communication, and more. Importantly, the Culture also addresses "What's in it for me?" by establishing the future view of life in a Vitalized organization.

A Vitalized Culture is one committed to becoming a progressive thinking, learning organization. A Culture committed to recognizing and expanding employee skills and potential, for greater contribution and collaboration across the organization anywhere, anytime. A Culture that believes in clear communication with all employees on every level and in every function. A Culture that clearly connects the employee, her job, and her importance to achieving the Vision and Mission for the company.

A Vitalized Culture consciously and intentionally reinforces the "why" for employees to work for your company and why they should feel excited and proud to do so. When employees experience an *aha moment* about where they fit, how they contribute their energy rises, commitment rises, and Vitality and loyalty soar.

A Vitalized Culture is proactive in identifying areas of stagnation, takes immediate action to resolve the situation, and instills confidence in employees that they are not alone. Leaders are visible, involved, and present. They value and mentor quality people-leadership on all levels and in all functions, regardless of formal education, and they recognize and celebrate success.

NOTES

Actions: _____

_____

_____

_____

_____

Call Whom: _____

_____

_____

_____

_____

By When: _____

_____

_____

_____

_____

*"We have to abandon the conceit that
isolated personal actions are going to solve this crisis.
Our policies have to shift."*

– AL GORE

CHAPTER 24

ENLIVENING YOUR POLICIES

CORPORATE POLICIES ARE THE FOURTH OF THE FOUR CORE leadership documents that set the direction and tone for an organization: Vision, Mission, Culture, and Policies. These documents are interrelated and interdependent. They support and reinforce one another.

The Vision sets the direction. The Mission introduces how the company plans to achieve the Vision. Together they provide the future-view, the roadmap of where you are going and how you are going to get there. The Culture defines the environment and provides the guidelines for the internal and external actions and behaviors of employees, customers, suppliers, and affiliates. These guidelines exemplify the organization's target qualities, which include: respect, honesty, trust, clarity, and teamwork.

Policies provide the details. They establish the "how to" and the boundaries, the consequences of not adhering to the Policies defined to help achieve Vision and Mission. Well-written Policies help establish and manage action, behavior, and communication between all elements of an organization.

Commonly known Policies provide guidelines for sourcing talent, employee benefits, work hours, salaries, negotiating contracts, financial methods, communication, and more. Policies are also instrumental in establishing boundaries for unacceptable behavior, and for defining procedures facilitating release of those who do not uphold the business' values.

Why Are Policies Important?

Policies provide a common understanding, a framework for greater trust, collaboration and opportunity. They help create a workplace where people are confident that they will be safe and supported to offer their best.

Unclear guidelines leave employee behaviors open to self-interpretation, creating confusion and conflicts that are hard to resolve. People manage their actions based on their own experience, their own criteria, and their own desire for gain. Without clear policies, no one is watching your quality control. Disagreements and lack of trust can undermine well-intended targets—from the inside out.

Well-written Policies require attention and intention. Attention to establish a common platform for interaction, and intention to create an environment where communication, collaboration, and Vitality thrives.

So, What's the Problem?

1. Policies are often out of date, perhaps written in another time and assumed to apply now. This laissez faire attitude toward Policies won't work today. Policies must be up to date for today's employees, today's needs and issues, today's market opportunities, and today's speed.

2. Most policies are presented in standard black-and-white documents with small print. Employees today are 80 percent visual learners, and almost 100 percent color communicators. Stoplights have three colors; credit cards have color-coding for credit levels. Movies, videos, games, and education are action and color.

3. Policies are generally communicated from a distance with little personal or departmental application. Remotely administered policies fail to manage chronic, pervasive negativity. Remote Policies don't watch to see whether employees are stagnant. They don't watch to see whether managers are people-leaders or stagnancy creators. And they don't determine whether an employee has a beneficial perspective of his or her job.

4. Inconsistent application of policies creates anger and negativity among the ranks.

5. Training policies are usually budget-limited and once-in-a-while events.

Make Policies Real, Relevant, and Rewarding

A progressive thinking, learning organization focuses on Vitalizing the Policies guiding it. Take your Policies out of the closet, rethink them, and make them visible and active.

Policies that are visible and active are:

1. Proactive: Encourage pro-active leadership as well as help manage behavior.
2. Current: Address current issues and opportunities.
3. Clear: Written plainly and easily to facilitate understanding.
4. Pertinent. They:
    a. Utilize language and concepts relevant to the audience
    b. Enable smooth, quality, respectful actions
    c. Help create a positive, interactive working environment
    d. Apply to both issues and opportunities
    e. Respect the original home-cultures and creeds of employees
    f. Apply to all employees, including managers and executives
    g. Help realize the potential and opportunity for all employees
5. Consistent:
    a. Convey stability of vision and leadership
    b. Reinforce "We are all in this together"
    c. Help build trust, teamwork, and collaboration
6. Visible and repeated

Policies as Beacons for Vitality

Policies that clearly and energetically support new Vitalize programs substantiate that the future is no longer "business-as-usual." They spark interest, and they encourage and require employee participation.

Policies can help clarify "it's a new day" by providing clear definition of new people-leadership requirements, respectful viable alternatives for those managers who don't want to participate; and by providing a framework for new experiential opportunity for those employees who want to participate more.

Start Vitalizing Your Policies—Simplified:

1. Initiate a Vitalize your Corporate Policies project to transform your business-as-usual Policies into declarations that this is a new day. Include your intention to become a progressive thinking, learning organization committed to Vitalizing Your Workforce as the new competitive edge.

2. Enlist your Corporate Vitality Team to participate in Vitality Policy development.

3. Formalize a cross-organization inquiry to understand your starting point:

    a. Who knows about the policies?

    b. Who knows what is in them?

    c. How visible are they?

    d. Are they easy to find?

    e. How are they shared? Communicated?

    f. How often are they communicated? By whom? For whom?

    g. How often are they updated? Who creates the updates?

    h. Do they include the intention to become a progressive thinking, learning organization dedicated to the Vitality of the business and all of its employees?

    i. Do they address leadership requirements for current managers? New managers?

    j. Do they include new hiring inquiry to identify incoming natural people-leaders regardless of education level or experience?

    k. Do they include the Policy of offering employee choice to expand their career opportunities based on personal initiative, thereby sharing the responsibility for their growth with their organization?

4. Cascade Your Policies

Cascading your Policies means sharing your Policy Guidelines with all levels and departments of the organization in a way that the level, department, and function can best understand them.

"Take the time to create a better way!"

Take the time not only to share the new Policy guidelines, but care enough to share them in the language of each department. The daily language of Sales is not the same daily language as Manufacturing. Appropriate language helps each department understand the Policies and how the Policies guide and support their work and their future.

Plan time to help employees understand how these new Vitality programs and policies provide ongoing opportunities to enhance their potential, interests, and contribution. Creating a better way to support and communicate the respective Policy guidelines helps restore employee trust and interest in working for your company, and it reminds them why they should be excited and proud to do so.

5. Enlist Your Natural People-Leaders

Enlist your people-leaders into your new policy communication team. Help them share Policy guidelines, Policy updates, and new initiatives in a way that benefits everyone involved. Mentor them to assess their departments' responses, share their questions, and clarify their concerns. Listen to their suggestions on how to improve communication and their departments' involvement. The natural people-leaders of a function speak that functional language. They know how to communicate and will be glad to work with you! That is Vitality!

CHAPTER 24
SUMMARY

WELL-WRITTEN AND CAREFULLY COMMUNICATED POLICIES can create a workplace where people feel safe and supported. Unfortunately, company Policies are often outdated, applied inconsistently, and insufficient to manage many employee issues. They often have limited scope and may restrict initiative. Take time to Vitalize your existing Policies to align with your new Vitalization goals.

Transformation from a business-as-usual organization to one full of Vitality requires declaring the intention to Vitalize your workforce. It requires creating policies that overtly support Vitality generating programs, support a positive Vitalized Culture, recognize employee participation, and ensure progressive learning.

Well-written policies that support Vitality programs enhance employee potential, help maintain employee interest and commitment, and reinforce why employees are proud to work for your company.

NOTES

Actions: _____

_____

_____

_____

_____

Call Whom: _____

_____

_____

_____

_____

By When: _____

_____

_____

_____

_____

"The trust of the people in the leaders reflects the confidence of the leaders in the people."

– PAUL FREIRE

CHAPTER 25

FINDING AND ACTIVATING YOUR REAL PEOPLE-LEADERS

IN CHAPTER 4, I INTRODUCED YOU TO JOHN AND THE IDEA and value of finding your natural people-leaders. John is a powerful energetic people leader in a truck-axle manufacturing plant. John does not have any advanced degrees or certifications, but John leads with an understanding that his department and the company can be more, and achieve more, than they are. He is an articulate communicator who reaches out to stagnant and reticent long-term employees in his group to gain their participation in designing a more efficient way to organize his shop floor and flow of materials. John has the wisdom and insight to reach his team where they are at the moment. He finds ways to identify and solve problems, and to exemplify the new work of his team to benefit the rest of the organization. John is a natural people-leader.

Finding and activating your natural people-leaders is imperative for any organization. Natural people-leaders work throughout your organization, largely silent, without recognition. These naturally talented employees can be a key to transforming your organization from stagnant to full of Vitality. They embody critical skill required for introducing, mentoring, and supporting new Vitality initiatives.

There are natural people-leaders everywhere—in any form of business or organization, in any age group, in every background, and every education level. In business organizations, employees are often stratified based on their educational achievements. This stratification does help to facilitate a common business language, and many people with advanced learning do have excellent people skills. However, these skills are often not regarded, prominent, or rewarded, and often the real human interaction of leadership is hidden.

Quality people-leadership skills are a critical ingredient for Vitalizing any organization. This gap is exponential and you need to pay attention. As twenty-somethings grow up with intense interactive internet-based lives, they enter the workforce where their strategies of motivation are often based on personal interest. The importance of consistent, clear motivational leadership and how to provide it for others is often missing.

> *"What is missing? The necessary, refined, and effective skills for employee leadership and motivation."*

If you are going to Vitalize your workforce, your organization and its leaders must fill this gap in spades. Your organization leadership must be the differentiator—exemplifying this critical training that is increasingly missing at home, compromised in schools, worsened on social media, and even eroded by the news. Where is a role model for positive, motivational leadership?

Finding and mentoring true people-leaders and cultivating hands-on leadership skills is mandatory—for you, your employees, and the company. You have a distinct opportunity to create your custom-designed team-of-teams and seed this vital skill throughout your organization. Natural people-leaders are part of your team.

What Are Natural People-Leaders?

Natural people-leaders are comfortable in their own skin, comfortable with who they are, and have little need to judge or criticize others. They can see the bigger picture and understand that there is more to an individual and situation than is apparent on the surface. They understand that individual potential is hiding and often reticent due to life experience, lack of confidence, or the employee's fear of losing his job if he fails. Natural people-leaders can calmly and effectively reach behind these veils of reticence to free employee potential.

Natural people-leaders have an innate, can-do attitude that enables them to listen well, be adaptable to changing situations, and be confident in adding their voices to better a situation. They enjoy opportunities to resolve issues that impede improvement and success. Natural people-leaders have an expanded perspective of their environment, and are ready, willing, and able to apply their initiative and potential on your behalf. They learn fast, apply what they learn rapidly, and are grateful for more. Find your natural people leaders and activate them!

Motivation is elemental to natural people-leaders. Retired General Stanley McChrystal knew that if his results were to change, his view of his own role had to change. As a result, he traded his historical "come to me for the answers" role for one of mentoring his people—let me help you learn how to find the answers and to make decisions yourself, and I'll support you. He is a natural people-leader.

Why Do You Want to Find and Activate Your Natural People-Leaders?

As you learn to measure the level of stagnancy and Vitality in your organization, you will become more aware of how many of your current managers are people-leaders, and how many are not—hence fueling stagnation. These findings may be uncomfortable, but they are more proof of the need to take action today to Vitalize your workforce.

Your natural people-leaders embody the spirit you want in your organization. Find them, recognize them, and activate them. Encourage them to be the first to learn about your new Vitality initiative. Inform them of your decision to implement a Chief Vitality Officer and team. Enlist them to be a proactive part of your new vertical and horizontal fabric of communication. Mentor them to help cascade your new Vision, Mission, and target Vitality Culture throughout your organization. Enlist them to be the first to learn Vitalize Issue Resolution and Problem-Solving techniques; Dynamic Delegation; and Energetic Mentoring. Mentor them to be proactive in your new Shared Learning Quality Circles to help train and mentor other employees to gain these critical skills for Vitalizing your organization.

Work with your Chief Vitality Officer Team to endorse natural people-leadership talents and skills. Add these skills as criteria for hiring new talent. Establish proven people-leadership skills as criteria for promotion to any management position; and establish lack of proven people-leadership skills as criteria for manager reassignment from people-leadership positions.

Vitalizing your Workforce is about people. You have employees who are natural people-leaders now, everywhere in your organization. Find, recognize, mentor, and engage them to help lead your organization for Vitality!

CHAPTER 25
SUMMARY

THE ABILITY TO LEAD PEOPLE IS INNATE IN SOME EMPLOYees, learned by others, and completely missing in even more. People-leaders are employees who have the natural ability to motivate and bring out the best in their colleagues. Natural people-leaders have excellent talents to lead in problem-solving, delegation, and mentoring. Importantly, they have natural initiative for teamwork with peers, management, and leadership.

Natural people-leaders are the gems in your organization. They are not necessarily well educated or academically adept, yet they possess an ability to connect, understand, motivate, and lead. They generally have a greater perspective of what needs to happen in a department for greater efficiencies, they participate well in planning cycles, and they stay on course for greater success.

A vital component of Vitalizing your workforce is to identify, recognize, and activate your natural people-leaders. Enlist them in your communications team to help cascade your Vision and Mission for a Vitalized organization and to be proactive support in your Vitalize initiatives. They are ready, willing, and able! That is Vitality!

NOTES

Actions: _____

_____

_____

_____

_____

Call Whom: _____

_____

_____

_____

_____

By When: _____

_____

_____

_____

_____

"Motivation, passion, and focus have to come from the top."

– KEVIN PLANK

SECTION 7
VITALIZE YOUR FOCUS

"Tell me how you measure me, and I will tell you how I will behave."

– ELI GOLDRATT

CHAPTER 26

MEASURING VITALITY IS AN IMPERATIVE

By Dr. James A. Robertson

IN CHAPTER 3, WE ESTABLISHED THAT MEASUREMENT CAN defuse toxic management dysfunction and demonstrated that it is vital to be able to measure Stagnation and Vitalization in order to Vitalize Your Workforce everywhere in your organization. In this chapter, we will explore this concept further.

1. **You cannot manage what you don't measure.**

    Peter Drucker said in essence that "If you can't measure it, you can't manage it... [or improve it]." This is a vital principle.

    In this book, we discussed a diversity of concepts and practices all directed at achieving the goal of Vitalizing Your Workforce. Many of these concepts and practices are universal and can be applied across the organization from end to end, leading to dramatic improvements in the organization's overall effectiveness, efficiency, and competitiveness.

    However, some issues require more focused treatment. It is one thing to diagnose the workforce's overall state of health as "Stagnant." The practicality of turning Stagnant situations into a Vitalized Workforce is another. The points that follow explore how we have come to understand the measurements necessary for treating Stagnation.

2. **"Tell me how you want me to behave and I will tell you how to measure me" is a fundamental principle.**

    Eli Goldratt coined the phrase *"Tell me how you measure me and I will tell you how I will behave."* In developing strategic measures and key performance indicators, we have come to understand that a fundamental corollary to this principle can be enunciated as the reverse—*"Tell me how you want me to behave and I will tell you how to measure me."*[58]

    When we examine the critical behaviors an organization is seeking to obtain from its employees in any particular department or function, and then we consult with the employees to develop measurements that support the employees delivering that behavior, we are taking a giant step.

    If you want your employees to be loyal and productive, you need to introduce measures that incentivize them to be loyal and believe in their opportunity with the organization. If you want to ensure they do not become dumbed down, you need to introduce incentive measures to energize and empower them.

    The Vitalize Your Workforce approach builds on this thinking with a series of bi-pole measures that span from the undesirable Stagnation attributes on the left to the desirable Vitalized attributes on the right:

Stagnant	0	1	2	3	4	5	6	7	8	9	10	Vitalized
Dying Organization					♦							Thriving Organization
Employee Malaise					♦							Vitalized / Agile-Flexible Employees
Management Not People Leaders					♦							Management Are People Leaders
Dumbed Down People					♦							Energized And Empowered People
Unhealthy Staff Turnover					♦							Loyalty
Negativity And Sabotage					♦							Positive And Collaborative
	-3σ		-2σ		-σ		0		+σ		+2σ +3σ	

3. **One-size-fits-all Human Resource treatment regimens are ineffective and destructive. Focused and precisely aligned treatment is essential.**

Many, possibly most, organizational improvement interventions adopt a one-size-fits-all treatment approach. All employees are subject to the same training, same motivational talks, or same measurements with no thought to the possibility that different employees have different personality profiles, different educational levels, different motivating factors, etc.

This one-size-fits-all approach is a key element in employee Stagnation. All employees are treated the same because it is too inconvenient to treat them differently and because managers have not thought it possible to treat them differently. By measuring individual Stagnation and Vitalization, the Vitalize Your Workforce approach ensures that remedial measures are focused and precisely aligned with the needs of different groups of employees.

4. **If you don't know the state of health of the patient, how do you prescribe the treatment?**

In medicine, considerable reliance is placed on simple measurements like pulse rate, blood pressure, etc. These simple measures give vital indications of the state of health or lack of health of the patient and, taken together, they point to likely diagnoses.

Stagnation and Vitalization are no different; they require measurement to establish the organization's state of health or lack of it, and, more specifically, the individual organizational entity or business unit as well as individual employees' state of health (stagnation versus vitalization). Correctly administered, these assessments allow accurate diagnosis of problem areas and also permit effective monitoring of the impact of corrective measures directed at delivering a high state of Vitalization. The absence of such measurements and the weaknesses of many forms of measurement have contributed to the poor success rate understanding and changing employee disengagement and stagnation.

5. **Effective analysis of any soft issue situation makes numeric measurement possible, practical, and valuable.**

One of the myths of organizational improvement is that it is possible to improve the overall state of health of organizations without effective measurements. On the other hand, where effective measurements are instituted, considerable value is unlocked in whatever area is being measured. The challenge is that in most areas relating to "soft issues," there is a mistaken belief that measurement is not possible and that subjective "gut feel" is the only available approach.

The fact is, with effective analysis of any particular soft issue, it is possible to define a set of measurements that enable the quantum of that issue to be measured and scaled, albeit on a somewhat more subjective basis than the determination of blood pressure or measurement of pulse rate.

6. **How do you measure Critical Concerns with regard to workforce vitality?**

Chapter 3: Real Change Requires Measurement exemplifies determination of Critical Concerns and other similar sets of parameters using an approach that comprises:

   a. Brainstorming issues

   b. Individually synthesizing critical (Pareto) factors

   c. Collaboratively combining critical factors

   d. Reducing each factor to a core statement

   e. Individually weighting the factors out of 100 percent to determine relative importance

   f. Discussing weights and combining arithmetically with executive over-ride

   g. Individually scoring the factors on a scale of 0 to 10 in terms of the factor's effectiveness of operation

   h. Discussing the scores and combining them arithmetically

   i. Determining gaps, analyzing them, and planning to close them

This approach can be applied to virtually any soft-issue domain that may be encountered in an organizational or individual life situation and is highly effective. While it may sound lengthy and time consuming, in practice, with the right software tools and an experienced facilitator, this process is quick and easy. We offer software and provide training for facilitators with regard to this approach.

The determination of Critical Concerns regarding Workforce Vitality is a key element of formulating an overall approach to addressing issues of Stagnation and Vitality. The result is a high-level, prioritized framework from which a structured plan can be developed. This plan will specify exactly what steps are to be taken to remedy a situation in a manner that is tailored to the individual organization.

7. **How do you measure individual employee vitalization?**

    To evaluate the organization's health, it is necessary to measure each employee's health in terms of stagnation versus vitalization.

    This measurement is done using my proprietary Individual Vitalization Assessment tool. Understanding each respondents' role in the organization allows this tool to aggregate vitality ratings for an individual at the most detailed level, through functional and geographical associations. Stakeholders can slice and dice the data in an unlimited number of ways to assess their organization's health and Vitality.

    Two assessments are conducted, one of the "Ideal Self" (the way the respondent views his or her behavior in an ideal work situation), and the second in terms of the "Current Self" (how the person feels required to act in his or her current job situation). These data provide input for sorting our each individual's score across the six essential bipolar categories listed in Figure 1 of this chapter.

    The data for each individual is associated with the organizational entity (business unit) the employee belongs to. This data is then fed into an enterprise visualization that allows the organization's state of health to be viewed graphically. This visualization allows focused executive prioritization of Vitalization campaign actions.

8. **How do you measure organizational entity vitalization?**

    To understand fully the Vitalization dynamics of any organization, it is necessary to assess the Vitalization status of every Organizational Entity that makes up the organization. This is done in two ways:

    a. By assessing the state of Vitalization of each and every employee using the Individual Assessment tool discussed in the previous section.

    b. By providing an Organizational Entity Assessment tool whereby executives and managers (and even customers and suppliers) can rate the state of health of any particular organizational entity (business unit) from an external perspective. Every department, every sub-department, and every branch can be collaboratively assessed by the leadership team and other stakeholders who have an informed opinion on that specific entity's health.

This provides two measures—a measure of the organizational entity's health as assessed by the employees assessing themselves and a second measure as observed by selected stakeholders. These two measures can then be compared and any gaps analyzed and addressed. This analysis can be particularly important if the staff says things are really bad and the broader stakeholder population see a different picture, or vice versa.

The Vitalize Organizational Entity Assessment enables rating of the entity's health on a scale of 0 to 10 where 0 = totally Stagnant (could not possibly be worse) and 10 = totally Vitalized (could not possibly be better).

These ratings are fed into an automated analysis that reports the relative levels of Stagnation versus Vitalization of the organizational entity in question:

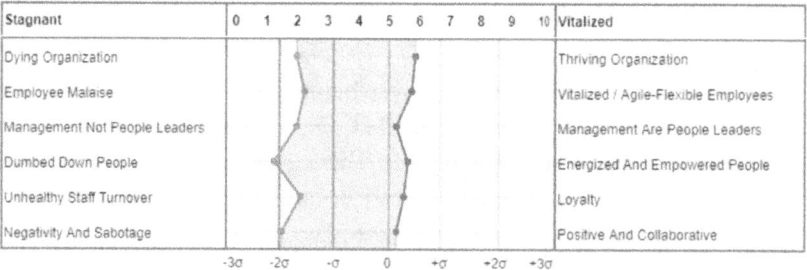

9. Engineered metrics are essential for effective diagnosis and treatment of workforce stagnation to vitalize your workforce

The above discussion encompasses a number of discrete metrics applicable to the discussion of Vitalizing Your Workforce.

These and other custom metrics developed during individual projects assist in bringing the rigorous engineering approach to measurement of so-called "soft issues" in general and to the process of Vitalizing Your Workforce in particular.

The use of measurement in all the dimensions of variability that occur in any enterprise are a vital component of the Vitalize Your Workforce approach.

CHAPTER 26
SUMMARY

A CRITICAL NEED FOR MEASUREMENT EXISTS IN MANAGING stagnation and creating vitality. This chapter describes the methods used to establish measurements for the key metrics necessary for an effective Vitalization initiative.

Measurement allows managers and consultants to clearly assess the state of play and establish performance improvement goals. Importantly, measurement allows one to focus energy on the critical pain points, understanding that 20 percent of prioritized effort and investment will deliver 80 percent of the value outcome.

NOTES

Actions: _____

_____

_____

_____

_____

_____

Call Whom: _____

_____

_____

_____

_____

By When: _____

_____

_____

_____

_____

_____

"To become truly great, one has to stand with people, not above them."

– CHARLES DE MONTESQUIEU

CHAPTER 27

FUTURE PERFECT IN A VITALIZED ORGANIZATION

THE CONCEPT OF "FUTURE PERFECT" CHALLENGES YOU TO look forward over an undetermined amount of time, freeing your intuition and imagination to surmise how a situation is likely to evolve—what it is likely to look like in the future…and what is likely to take place between now and then.

Today, many organizations are in a crisis—a crisis of stagnation likely to cripple them on many levels if they continue without defining a culture, action, and result they really want and go for it. Complacency is not an option. They can celebrate what they think they were yesterday, or today, but tomorrow, collapse may be imminent in the absence of dynamic new action.

Looking at your organization today requires strength and resolve. It takes strength and resolve to look in the mirror and be honest about what you see. Some of you will and some of you won't. That is a choice for sure. If you do look in the mirror, however, you can sharpen your understanding of what stagnation means in your organization—what toll it is taking where and with whom.

You can sharpen your understanding of the scale of thinking required to change your paradigm for a more fluid, fertile future, and to facilitate focus on critical issues, through honest assessment of Vitality and stagnancy in your organization today.

Let's look in the mirror together. Although every organization has positive and negative characteristics, a helpful starting point is to compare what you consider to be your employees' most debilitating characteristics with what you consider to be their best, most desired characteristics. This comparison produces a gap. The gap provides a variety of indicators for your planning, designing, and decision selection.

A Stagnant Organization	A Thriving Organization
Employee malaise	**Energized and Empowered People**
Lack of interest in the job	Feel extra work and effort is worthwhile
Lack of interest in the organization	Willing and encouraged to expand their: a) capabilities b) potential c) contribution
Lack of interest in learning anything new	
Low morale, low energy	
Believe nothing will change, i.e., there is nothing here for us anymore except the benefits	Go the extra mile
No alternative but to ride it out or leave	Do not watch the clock
	Talk about their work enthusiastically to anyone who will listen

A Stagnant Organization	A Thriving Organization
Management who are not people leaders	**Management who *are* people leaders**
Indifferent	Understand and believe that organizations thrive on desire, interest, and potential of people
Little connection with their people	Have and offer natural people skills
Focused on own job at expense of subordinates	Have natural communication skills
Remote to employee potential and interests Treat people as numbers—told what to do	Engage people in: a) problem solving b) delegation c) mentoring d) idea generation e) planning new programs, products, and services f) develop their own work opportunities
	Are natural leaders
	Build trust, teamwork, positive outlook, positive attitude. Look out for the future of employees in their charge.
	Employees want to be around them, follow them, and work increases

A Stagnant Organization	A Thriving Organization
Dumbed Down People	**Vitalized/Agile-Flexible Employees**
No future	Enjoy their jobs
No learning, no growth	Excited about their futures
No reward for creativity or initiative	Learning more and more all the time
Joined with enthusiasm, then…	Expanding their value and capabilities to contribute
	Highly motivated
	Team players
	High energy and enthusiasm
	Empowered and quick to delegate and accept delegation
	Flexible in response to daily demands of their jobs
Unhealthy Staff Turnover	**Loyalty**
Leave a job for negative reasons	Unswerving loyalty
Leave a manager for negative reasons	Dedication and commitment to the organization
Leave an organization for negative reasons	Dedication and commitment to the leaders of the organization

A Stagnant Organization	A Thriving Organization
High negative bottom-line impact	Respect for, and interest in, supporting strong leadership
High "I've had enough" factor	Provide willing extra effort to support the organization and its leaders
Negativity and Sabotage	**Positive and Collaborative**
Show poor attitude	Positive (good, willing, productive) attitude
Do not communicate	Communicate
Keep things to themselves	Proactive
Block or negate positive initiatives	Share ideas
Bad mouth colleagues or superiors	Work with others easily and productively toward common goals because they want to do more, be more, and become more…together
Detriment to the organization—slander inside and out with customers and suppliers	Good communication about the organization
Impede improvement	
Hamper success	
Dying Organization	**Thriving Organization**
Declining order size	Glowing with creativity, collaboration, new ideas

A Stagnant Organization	A Thriving Organization
Low interest to join by top talent	Innovative and creative
Withering customer base	Highly competitive
Low or no new product development	Growing constantly
Losing investors	Personnel work as mutually supportive teams
No strategic vision, no plan for the future	Personnel give one another mutual support
Surviving day by day	Highly differentiated

This contrast exemplifies the need for extraordinary transformation of leadership thinking and the direction to re-form organizations. Without addressing this fundamental change first, you have little with which to work.

Seven Considerations as You Reach for Future Perfect:

1. **Energized and Empowered People**

   What do the photographs of the people within the "Top 25 Companies to Work For" show us? Smiles. Confidence. Challenge. Learning and Support. These images have values that cannot be photo-shopped onto the bodies in the frames. They really are that happy. Of course, they are real people with real problems working for a real company that is worried everyday whether or not they are succeeding. That part of business will not change. But the people in our workforces have changed a great deal. If your workforce is not committed to your company's Vision, Mission, Culture, and Policies, then you are trying to hold water in your bare hands. A Vitalized Workforce is Energized and Empowered. Its members are not perfect or easy or abnormal. They know what's in it for you, and they know what's in it for them—because you pay attention and provide the structure, training, mentoring, and Integrated Incentives for continual opportunity, recognition, and respect for their potential.

When the Millennials first came on the scene, their vocal question "What's in it for me?" was seen as an impertinent challenge to the status quo. It was considered arrogant and a worrisome defiance to the usual ability to maintain silent control. We know now that we should thank them.

The Vitalized organization now anticipates this question from any employee, anywhere in the organization. It creates a consistent, progressive thinking, learning environment where new opportunities to expand employee skills and perspectives is the norm.

This opportunity is no longer "free" however. Employee skill and human potential evolution is now a partnership between the company and the employee. The organization establishes continual learning and skill application experience, tracks employee participation, and ensures constructive progressive opportunity for its employees.

The employee is responsible for participating in the progressive thinking, learning culture, and programs. The premise is earned opportunity. Employees can earn new learning opportunities any time, as fast as they want to and as fast as they can through demonstrating greater and greater participation and reach. This is shared learning at its best. A win-win for both the company and the employee.

Once this door is opened for employees to reach for their own potential and they begin to realize the value of a Vitalized Culture, "What's in it for me" is always within their reach for new opportunities and challenges.

2. **Vitality Leadership as a Critical Operations Requirement (Chief Vitality Officer)**

There is a new sheriff in town, the Chief Vitality Officer, and he (or she) wants you to jump farther and fly higher than you ever thought possible. Whether we consider a player/coach model or a best practices design, recognized and celebrated role models inspire the increased performance of people. This function is separate and distinct from Human Resources or the Talent Development Group. The Chief Vitality Officer is responsible for creating, overseeing, and evolving a unique and tailor-made Vitality program for the company.

The Chief Vitality Officer is accountable for systematically and peacefully evolving an organization from business-as-usual to a confident, Vitalized organization. The Vitality Leadership Team respects existing functional arenas (manufacturing, accounting, product development, etc.), simultaneously determines as many points of employee stagnation as possible, and helps define clear and sustainable solutions that inspire organizational nimbleness and ingenuity at every level of authority. The Chief Vitality Officer is also responsible for establishing and leading the company toward achievement of the Vitality Leadership Award. Striving toward the Vitality Leadership Award is what separates progressive companies from those not ready to evolve.

Organizations that appoint a Chief Vitality Officer attract new business that is looking for Vitality suppliers, partners, or affiliates. Such organizations recognize and interact with other organizations and trade, labor, and professional associates that respect and embrace the Vitality Leadership Award. They establish criteria for hiring top Vitality talent and attract top talent with proven Vitality Leadership experience to accelerate advancement toward the Vitality Leadership Award and its inherent competitive market advantage.

3. **Strategic Measurements (Organizational)**

Whether you are navigating the ocean or the worldwide marketplace, you can't get where you are going without knowing first where you are. Measurement is the vital key to any course change or adaptation within your business. A Vitalized organization measures classic values such as productivity, retention, attendance absenteeism, and employee turnover (planned and unplanned) while comparing static (non-participation-related) data.

However, numbers are not people, and people are the drivers of success or failure in any organization. The Vitalized organization has metrics that measure leadership performance toward Vitalization goals. These goals include consistent oversight of programs that enlist employees in problem-solving, cross-training, and other Vitalization skills. Performance relative to these goals is tracked by applying the proprietary measurement tools of Vitalize Your Workforce. These tools, used in conjunction with Vitalized Vision and Mission Statements, a purpose-built working Culture, and dynamic organizational Policies, yield human collaboration opportunities that organically accelerate workforce productivity.

4. **Vitality Metrics (Human Capital Potential)**

The core attributes of Vitalized Workforces are employees who are energized, motivated, empowered, and equipped to take the organization to new heights. Vitalization includes the current concepts of agility and flexibility, but it goes way beyond these concepts, driving personal initiatives for contribution and personal skill evolution.

Considering the opposing force of stagnation, these attributes provide expanding ways of thinking and acting for ongoing new, creative, and collaborative outcomes. Enhancement of these attributes requires tracking of training and evolution of both natural and learned skills and talents to ensure progressive versus once-in-a-while training.

As workplace boundaries have blurred, so have the lines between personal and professional interests. Embracing these changes in boundaries and providing new leadership initiatives allows for a more holistic approach to growing natural leadership.

> *"When human potential is recognized and its power released to experience itself, it thrives and expands."*

Vitalized organizations that capitalize on this powerful potential experience more employee buy-in, more enthusiasm, stronger attendance, reduction in negative behaviors, increased organic learning, loyalty, and economic and social reward.

5. **Increased Shareholder Value and Profitability**

All organizations are held to standards of Value and Profitability. The ability to utilize and evolve human potential as a primary asset to achieve profitability and ROI is a primary goal and result of the Vitalized organization. Sustainable business resiliency and accelerated action is developed through setting standards and rewarding workforce ability to plan for, and respond to, fast-changing market conditions and opportunities.

Shareholders, investors, and employees vote with their checkbooks. Today's marketplace is very personal in ways unimaginable a few years ago. The goal of a company today is not to just to make a profit, but to make a profit in a manner acceptable to all stakeholders.

Increasingly, executives who lead for and with Vitality while respecting, supporting, and rewarding their workforces create value and profitability. Fundamentally, a Vitalized organization is one that is more effective and, therefore, more profitable, delivering enhanced return on investment.

6. Integrated Team Leadership Philosophy

The Information Age has radically redefined the parameters of corporate leadership and governance with significant impact on traditional top-down leadership as an effective management tool. Factory-style production is vastly compromised and complicated by the speed and volume of information available democratically to a worldwide workforce. Respect, collaboration, recognition, and bilateral communication characterize the Vitalized Organization. Therefore, leadership, as a method and coachable behavior, is now illustrated by Vitality and committed teams of people working in concert with other teams of dynamic organizational players.

In his book Team of Teams, retired General Stanley McChrystal describes a large and complex organization operated on the same basis as the operation of individual teams. It's a situation where teams operate together as a larger team, and larger teams, in turn, operate together as an even larger team.

This teams-made-up-of-teams approach identifies mechanisms for operation and management in organizations that fully exploit the capabilities of the individuals and groups that make up the organization. This approach is an essential component of the Vitalize Your Workforce approach to management.

These teams of empowered employees are recognized by a mechanism where power, potential, and capability are shared by all employees to make decisions, share learning, support resilience after mistakes, and take on greater challenges. These highly productive behaviors grow and become stronger because the team members know they can trust each other.

This trust is purpose-built by cross-training, cross-awareness, and universal perspectives that allow for cooperative impact activities and decisions. They have greater confidence in their own decision-making and exhibit the Vitality, agility, and flexibility to apply constructive inputs without being territorial. They can reach up, down, and across for information and support.

Teams of this nature like to be measured. They recognize that measurement is an asset and not a threat. Because they are forward acting and forward thinking, they seek the efficiencies of measurement to gauge what they are doing for the organization. This has an unexpected and highly valued result: the team has fun accomplishing greater goals and growing into new knowledge, capabilities, and recognition. These value-based behaviors trigger greater independent problem solving, spontaneous and effective training activities, and greater identification of individuals to the team success.

7. **Vitality Circles**

Historically, Quality Circles designed for manufacturing offer a level of logic that helped redefined the top-down management of the previous century. Quality Circles are credited specifically with catapulting aging and obsolete industries and companies into the forefront of their markets. Key to this form is the breaking of hierarchal management. Essentially, Quality Circles create systematic assessment, communication, and collaboration on a company-wide basis, continually and peacefully.

Vitalize Your Workforce utilizes this proven construct for teamwork in a new way with Vitality Circles. Vitality Circles follow and reinforce on-site and online training of core skill requirements, providing a local forum for more personal encouragement for experiential practice of the skill and mentoring. Vitality Circles required within functions promote direct application of the required skills to that function, rather than offering traditional by-the-hour course instruction with little or no follow-up.

Importantly, function-specific Vitality Circles enable peer dialog and shared learning in a function's language that everyone understands. They enable mentored experimentation and practice of the new skills in their own environment to assure assimilation of the new learning as a natural expansion of their capability—together.

This organic learning is the key to addressing internal company challenges and emerging market issues quickly and easily. The Vitality Circle approach to training also enables rapid collaboration between quality circles in other functions or departments because all employees now have high proficiency in common skills required for excellence in communication, teamwork, idea sharing, and problem solving.

Vitality Circle training and practice enable systematic organization evolution to a new Vitalized culture where the Vitalized employees are continually empowered to participate and contribute with more and more of their innate potential, individually and collectively. This empowered role is fuel that accelerates employee desire to improve, excel, and accomplish measurable organizational goals and objectives. And it is the fuel to evolve your employees' potential as the primary asset to achieve future, sustainable profitability and ROI.

The overall future state of a Vitalized organization is one that is highly competitive, highly effective, highly efficient, and functions at a level way beyond the previous century's established norms and practices. We are talking about an organization that delivers on its true potential in fulfilling and empowering ways that make it a pleasure to be its shareholder, and a pleasure to be its employee.

CHAPTER 27
SUMMARY

THE CONCEPT OF "FUTURE PERFECT" CHALLENGES YOU TO look forward over an undetermined amount of time, freeing your intuition and imagination to surmise how a situation is likely to evolve. What it is likely to look like in the future…and what is likely to take place between now and then.

Today, many organizations are in a crisis—a crisis of stagnation that is likely to cripple them on many levels if they continue without defining a culture, action, and result they really want and go for it. Complacency is not an option. They can celebrate what they think they were yesterday, or today, but tomorrow collapse may be imminent in the absence of dynamic new action.

You can sharpen your understanding of the scale of thinking required to change your paradigm for a more fluid, fertile future through honest assessment of Vitality and stagnancy in your organization today. This comparison produces a gap. The gap provides a variety of indicators for your planning, designing, and decision selection. This contrast exemplifies the need for extraordinary transformation of leadership thinking and the direction to re-form organizations. Without addressing this fundamental change first, you have little with which to work.

Seven Considerations as You Reach for Future Perfect:

1. Energized and Empowered People
2. Vitality Leadership as a Serious Leadership Requirement (Chief Vitality Officer)
3. Strategic Measurements (Organizational)
4. Vitality Metrics (Human Capital Potential)
5. Increased Shareholder Value and Profitability
6. Integrated Team Leadership Philosophy
7. Vitality Circles

NOTES

Actions: _____

_____

_____

_____

_____

Call Whom: _____

_____

_____

_____

_____

By When: _____

_____

_____

_____

_____

"Employee disengagement is at epidemic levels."

– GOOGLE, 32,000 WEBPAGES

CHAPTER 28

THE CRITICAL FACTORS IN VITALIZING YOUR WORKFORCE

By Dr. James A Robertson

A SEARCH ON GOOGLE FOR "EMPLOYEE DISENGAGEMENT IS at epidemic levels" at the time of this writing returned about 32,000 results. "Employee disengagement" alone returned 68,500 results with reports going back over a decade—this count is the number of web pages with that exact phrase—clearly employee disengagement is a problem.

Steve Crabtree, in a post dated October 8, 2013 at www.gallup.com, reported that the latest Gallup survey at that time reported that only 13 percent of employees worldwide were engaged at work. Other articles support this. An average of 85 percent of personnel are still disengaged.

So, we know there is a problem, but despite widespread publicity and innumerable consulting firms working full time to address the problem, it appears the problem is getting worse, not better.

So, what is going wrong? What isn't working?

First, the diagnosis is faulty. The problem is "stagnation"—a more far-reaching phenomenon than "disengagement"—so the world is treating a symptom and not the cause. In fact, it is true to say that in 2017, "disengagement is yesterday's story," "disengagement is passé."[59]

More critically, attempts to address the problem, however defined, are failing to address the real issues in a competitive business improvement.

The author of this chapter is an engineer by training and has been involved in strategic business improvement since 1981 and consulting in that field since 1989. He has investigated dozens of failed and sub-optimal strategic improvement projects and initiatives and successfully assisted clients to turn many of those situations around.

In analyzing these failures and subsequent successes, he developed a suite of "Factors Causing Failure" together with a suite of the "Critical Factors for Success." These factors apply to any strategic organizational improvement project, such as a Vitalize Your Workforce project, and are presented below.

You may ask what engineering has to do with a "soft" topic like employee stagnation. The answer is simple. Vitalizing employees, after possibly years of stagnation, to bring about enduring and sustainable business improvement is a largely intangible and invisible endeavor. At the same time, stagnation as a "soft" issue is reported to be costing the US economy over $500 billion per year. This impact can hardly be described as "soft"!

Engineers are trained to design and build things that work reliably and sustainably all the time. That is exactly what we are looking for here—an approach to Vitalizing a Stagnant Workforce that works reliably and sustainably all the time.

With that in mind, we would like to present an overview of an Engineering Approach to add some concrete thinking to soft issues.

Engineers apply a structured approach to make things work consistently and reliably, day in and day out. We take it for granted that our roads, railways, buildings, factories, etc. will be built and will work. Yes, sometimes there are time and cost overruns, but the level of technical failure, which is at epidemic proportions in the business improvement arena, is entirely unthinkable.

The engineering Factors for Success comprise two elements: 1) factors that cause failure that must be managed out of the project, and 2) factors for success that must be managed in. Managing the factors causing failure is one of the key differentiators in the Vitalize Your Workforce approach discussed here.

Following are the headlines of this approach.

Succeed by Engineering Against Failure

A fundamental principle of engineering is that engineers do *not* design for success; they design against failure. In other words, "engineers do *not* design bridges to stand up; they design bridges *not* to fall down."

It is a fundamental principle that a well-designed system that does not fail will succeed. Yet success is achieved by preventing failure. Engineers study the principles of "factor of safety" and ""probability of failure" as elemental concepts that are consistently applied to all they do. The percentages in the following chart "The Factors Causing Business Improvement Failure,"[60] are indicative of the relative importance of these factors in our experience and are also roughly indicative of the relative frequency of these factors in causing sub-optimal and failed outcomes:

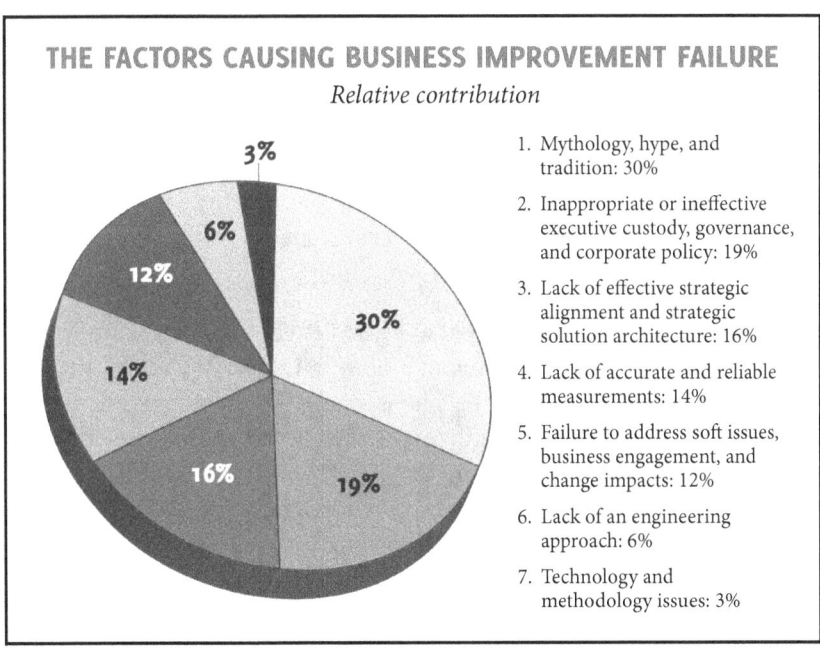

THE FACTORS CAUSING BUSINESS IMPROVEMENT FAILURE
Relative contribution

1. Mythology, hype, and tradition: 30%
2. Inappropriate or ineffective executive custody, governance, and corporate policy: 19%
3. Lack of effective strategic alignment and strategic solution architecture: 16%
4. Lack of accurate and reliable measurements: 14%
5. Failure to address soft issues, business engagement, and change impacts: 12%
6. Lack of an engineering approach: 6%
7. Technology and methodology issues: 3%

1. Mythology, Hype, and Tradition—30 percent

   This is a huge subject. The business improvement industry is rich in tradition. Unfortunately, often a silent wish is that continuing business as usual will produce different results. The Vitalize Your Workforce approach demonstrates different thinking. One key is incorporating the Engineering Approach as a cornerstone of the Vitalize Your Workforce consulting methodology.

2. **Inappropriate or Ineffective Executive Custody, Governance, and Corporate Policy—19 percent**

    The governance and policies of major business improvement projects are frequently flawed. Strategic employee-related projects are often delegated to the Human Resources manager to run. The chief executive is actually the custodian of the integrated view of the business and is, therefore, the only person with the mandate and insight to give direction to the project.

3. **Lack of Effective Strategic Alignment and Strategic Solution Architecture—16 percent**

    If you have not read Chapter 20: Discovering the Strategic Essence of Your Organization, you might consider doing so now. As the examples in that chapter demonstrate, clear understanding of the enterprise's strategic essence is vital to successful high value Vitalization investments. Effective strategic alignment is, therefore, a core component of any Vitalization project.

4. **Lack of Accurate and Reliable Measurements—14 percent**

    Drucker is reported to have said that "If you can't measure it, you can't improve it." Measurement of soft issues is vital to managing them and to addressing phenomena like employee stagnation. Vitalize Your Workforce utilizes proprietary computer-based assessment instruments to measure Stagnation and Vitalization.

    A major distinction between the average business improvement project and the average engineering project is that engineering systems are designed for predictable consistency. Business improvements, even those that are well planned and adopt a program management approach, often experience dramatic variations in value and performance delivered.

5. **Failure to Address Soft Issues, Business Engagement, and Change Impacts—12 percent**

    "Change management? We *do* that!" Every project has a change management component. Problems arise when these changes are directed, not well thought out from the employee perspective, and often poorly executed. This combination of factors makes resentment and stagnation worse, not better.

6. **Lack of an Engineering Approach—6 percent**

    The reason lack of Engineering Approach has such a low score is that the other aspects of failure above have greater impact. The rigor, discipline, and design against failure of the engineering approach must permeate *every* element of the project.

7. **Technology Issues—3 percent**

    Technology is generally not the problem today. When it appears to be the problem, it is generally the consequence of the other factors discussed above that manifest in bad technology decisions.

The Critical Factors for Success[60]

Having managed failure out of the project, we can now focus on success.

Managing against failure requires a Senior Project Team Member who has key project responsibility to manage against failure. This Senior Project Team Member sits in project meetings and listens for the factors causing failure, identifies them, and manages them off the project. They review all project documentation, ranging from the project definition through to ensuring clarity and practicality in presentations to the Board.

The factors, weighted as above, are:

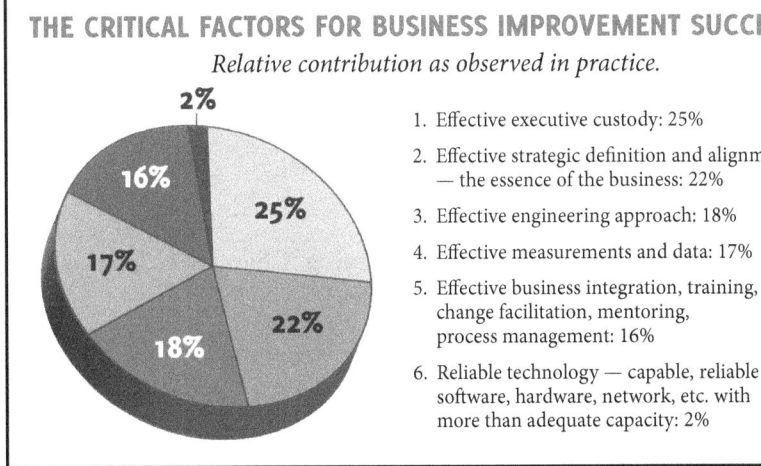

THE CRITICAL FACTORS FOR BUSINESS IMPROVEMENT SUCCESS
Relative contribution as observed in practice.

1. Effective executive custody: 25%
2. Effective strategic definition and alignment — the essence of the business: 22%
3. Effective engineering approach: 18%
4. Effective measurements and data: 17%
5. Effective business integration, training, change facilitation, mentoring, process management: 16%
6. Reliable technology — capable, reliable software, hardware, network, etc. with more than adequate capacity: 2%

1. **Effective Executive Custody—25 percent**

   Assign the right organizational executive in charge of the project. Ideally, there should be a strong single individual as client project team leader. There should be an equally strong single individual on the consultant side as project team leader.

2. **Effective Strategic Definition and Alignment— the Essence of the Business—22 percent**

   Integrate the Strategic Essence into the project's entire fabric. Do not allow any person who does not demonstrate a deep and empathetic understanding of the Strategic Essence to give overall direction to any aspect of the project. Capture the Strategic Essence in every aspect of what is undertaken.

3. **Effective Engineering Solution Design and Implementation Approach—18 percent**

   Introduce the rigors of standard engineering practice into your project. The Problem is that most engineers do *not* understand business improvement and business improvement people often do *not* understand engineers, so they miss each other totally if you are not careful. The Vitalize Your Workforce team has invested substantial amounts of time and money learning how to bring Engineering Discipline and methods to the business improvement industry.

4. **Effective Measurement and Data—17 percent**

   Well-designed measurements are an essential component of any Vitalize Your Workforce project.

5. **Effective Business Integration, Training, Change Facilitation, and Process Specification—16 percent**

   Business integration, training, helping people to change, including mentoring and mentoring management software, are all vital elements of an effective Vitalization project.

6. **Reliable Technology—2 percent**

    Reliable technology is essential, but it is only an issue if it fails to deliver. Do not cut corners.

Conclusion

If you address all the above in conjunction with a high-quality team that knows the methodology and a high-quality business team that knows the business, you will succeed. Additionally, if you treat your Vitalize investment as one of the most far-reaching projects that your business is likely ever to undertake, you will find that application of these principles will have a huge beneficial impact.

CHAPTER 28
SUMMARY

THE ORGANIZATIONAL IMPROVEMENT INDUSTRY IS RIFE with failed and sub-optimal project outcomes. Employee lack of engagement has been a focus for decades, and yet, it becomes worse not better.

This chapter discusses some elements of an Engineering Approach to Vitalizing the workforce and reports the Critical Factors that give rise to project failure and the Critical Factors for success.

These diagnostic indicators have been researched and understood over a considerable time period and provide a robust framework for any organizational improvement project. They are central to our thinking with regard to the Vitalize Your Workforce approach.

NOTES

Actions: _____

_____

_____

_____

_____

Call Whom: _____

_____

_____

_____

_____

By When: _____

_____

_____

_____

_____

"Just as in sports a coach needs a team of good players to win, an organization needs a team of good leaders to lead."

– JOHN MAXWELL

A FINAL NOTE

LEADING FOR VITALITY GUARANTEES SUCCESS

NOW WHAT? NOW THAT YOU HAVE READ *VITALIZE YOUR Workforce*, you know the difference between stagnant and Vitalized organizations. You have learned the causes of pervasive stagnation. You are more aware of the factors inherent in keeping your employee enthusiasm at a disinterested state, and how to transform your employee commitment, hope, and energy into Vitality to meet future change and opportunity. You learned that you *can* measure the level of stagnation and vitality anywhere in your organization, and you *can* utilize these comparative measurements to establish priorities and transformation initiatives for your organization.

You learned that there *are* ready, customizable programs for you to help evolve your workforce from stagnant to Vitalized. You learned how Shared Learning across the organization increases communication and collaboration and creates Vitality. You know why you need to find your natural people-leaders and mentor them to help with communication and employee motivation.

You now know the necessity of creating a permanent Chief Vitality Officer function reporting directly to the Chief Executive, directly accountable for instilling, managing, and expanding the fabric of Vitality Leadership across the organization. You know the imperative to set a clear new Vision and Mission for Corporate Vitality. You know the imperative to cascade and communicate your intentions effectively and continually to become a Vitality Leader to all levels, departments, functions, and employees in a way they can hear and understand. And you definitely know the imperative and competitive advantages to becoming a Vitality Leader in the marketplace.

And that's not all. You also learned:

- The ideal future state for your employees and the critical factors to Vitalize Your Workforce
- How to create energetic mentoring relationships among employees
- How to provide meaningful employee recognition and celebration, so employees truly share in being appreciated contributors to your company
- How to attract top-level talent looking for a Vitality Company with progressive policies and a reputation for superior performance

If you feel a burning desire to create an emboldened Vision and Mission to become a Vitality Award organization, you already know that a strong new competitive edge is yours with the decision. You know you can achieve an increasingly robust, resilient company with a Vitalized workforce that is ready to face whatever future may bring.

I encourage you to contact me and share what you liked about my book, and how we can improve it for the next printing. More importantly, tell me about yourself, your business challenges, and your organization's obstacles and adversities so I can stand with you and help.

In fact, I am offering you a complimentary, no obligation sixty-minute consultation by phone, Skype, Zoom, or in person (if convenient) to answer your questions and help me understand how I can assist you.

Please contact me. My email address is CEO@VitalizeYourWorkforce.com or visit our website at www.VitalizeYourWorkforce.com to book your free consultation.

If you apply the Vitalize wisdom, knowledge, experience, skills, strategies, and techniques to your organization, you will achieve what the title and subtitle promise—you will Conquer the Crisis of Employee Stagnation. You will be able to see the crisis of stagnation in your competitors more clearly and accelerate your competitive advantage so you do much more than just survive. You will secure your future with Vitality Leadership and commit yourself to a Vitality workforce as a new competitive edge.

I wish you great success. This new accelerating world needs all of us, Vitalized and ready!

Your friend,

Margot Murphy

VITALIZE YOUR WORKFORCE VOCABULARY

3.5 second attention span: The human attention span today, resulting from accelerating technologies, video games, commercialism, hyper-media interference, and more.

ATD: Association for Talent Development

Agile: A commonly used term for business improvement in response to employee lack of engagement. Vitality is a superset of Agility and is the core focus of this book. Vitality embraces a wide range of issues, including the emotional and mental health of employees in a workplace context by dealing with root causes of factors that give rise to employee stagnation. Vitality is a concept that in itself is much wider than "lack of engagement" or "agility."

Appreciation: Recognition of the quality, value, and significance of people and their positive actions.

Appreciation Files: In-office files created for each employee to collect evidence of the good, constructive actions taken by employees while employed by an organization. These files are managed by a supervisor and their progressive use overseen by the Chief Vitality Officer. They are the useful property of the employee (versus HR files that belong to the "company"). They are accessible to the employee to support his or her interviewing for new work or volunteer opportunities within or outside the organization. Related terms are:

- **Employee Appreciation Files:** Appreciation files with formal designation of the employee's name and year for the collection of Appreciations. The overt employee name provides important personal employee awareness and recognition. The year requires supervisor awareness of the need to support all employees, every year.

- **Appreciation File Program:** A formal program, recognized, implemented, and overseen by organization leadership to pro-actively provide encouragement, confidence, and life-work balance for each employee. A method to acknowledge an employee as a beneficial part of your organization, and a person with a future worth supporting, inside or outside your organization.

Appreciative Inquiry: 1. The act of exploration and discovery. 2. To ask questions; to be open to seeing new potentials and possibilities. From *A Positive Revolution in Change: Appreciative Inquiry* by David L. Cooperrider and Diana Whitney.

Assessment: The use of Vitalize Software Tools to assess the Vitality of the individuals, groups, and organizational elements (business units) of a company or organization.

Balance/Work-Life Balance: Focus on building employee confidence in their ability to enhance their contribution at work, support their families at home, and provide greater contribution as leaders in their communities. Recognizing and supporting the individual as a contributor to the whole of life, not just his or her job.

Business Unit (Organization Element): The component of an organization that is being modeled or managed in the Vitalize Your Workforce Process.

Capacity to Do Better: Capacity is the ability or power to do, experience, or understand something. "Capacity" as related to "potential": Having or showing the capacity to become or develop into something greater in the future. Potential is the latent qualities or abilities that may be developed and lead to future success or usefulness.

Cascading Communication: Cascading communication is the passing down of information to each level and function in the language and manner most easily understood by that department or function. Each function has its own vernacular. Accounting "language" is not the same as the "language" in shipping and receiving. Creating ways to cascade communication effectively in the "language" pertinent to the listener helps emphasize the information's importance to employee's job; and helps build the connection and confidence of employees about their importance to the organization's success. Cascading communication throughout the organization ensures all employees receive the messages, not just the few at the top.

Cascading Your Key Leadership Statements (Vision, Mission, Culture, Policies): Cascading of your Vision, Mission, Culture, and Policies is vital to your employees feeling connected to your organization, and to building their confidence in their *own* futures while working for you. Employee Vitality depends on linking employee value in their *own* lives to your vision for building the value of your business.

Contributing Mission Statement: A sub-Mission Statement developed specifically for a department, function, group, or job that:

- Connects the importance of that department's work directly to the company Mission Statement.
- Provides visibility and respect for the employee and department contribution.

Collaborative Sense of Purpose: 1) Motivation for employees to cooperate harmoniously to achieve a common goal, and share the recognition and reward. 2) The shared reason to include, communicate, train, mentor, accomplish, and achieve a common goal(s).

A collaborative sense of purpose includes all aspects of productivity: work planning, assignment, timeline, reason for each job, communication, skill training required/provided, mentoring, target results, measurements for success and more.

Credit Card Model: An incentive model recognized by all employees, globally, communicating various levels of incentives; it clarifies actions and behaviors required to reach increasingly progressive levels or rewards.

Critical Concerns Process: The Vitalize Your Workforce process employed at the commencement of a Vitalize Your Workforce engagement to assess the critical issues facing the organization as evaluated by the Executive team or other groups of organization employees.

Chief Vitality Officer: The Executive responsible for implementing the Vitalize principles and methods across the entire organization—must be a C-Level appointment.

Cross-Training: Cross-training relates to offering employees the opportunity to learn about the work performed and methods used in allied functions, departments, and branches. Cross-training provides a variety of different work opportunities, experiences, and skill exercises that build strength and flexibility in thought and action that working alone doesn't utilize or build. Cross-training increases flexibility in thinking, increases openness to share ideas, increases individual confidence, and builds increasing interest and enjoyment in collaboration anywhere, any time.

Culture Statement: One of the four Core Leadership Statements required to focus an organization to achieve a set of desired goals. A clearly defined Culture Statement defines the Values inherent in the leadership-employee relationship, peer-to-peer relationship; organization to supplier/customer and investor relationships.

"Dead-End" Managers: Managers who have little or no interest in leading, motivating, or supporting the employees under their care. Dead-End Managers may help create stagnant, disengaged employees because they have little or no training or experience to lead. These managers require training and mentoring to exercise and build their leadership "muscle." Other Dead-End Managers have no interest and don't want to lead. Their own personal job and promotion is most important. These managers are serious blocks to your employee vitality, and they breed employee stagnation every moment they are in a people-leadership position.

Delegate: There are two definitions of "delegate." One is a verb: to delegate; and one is a noun: a delegate. Both definitions are valuable for Dynamic Delegation™. To delegate means to pass on, hand on/over, or turn over a task or responsibility to another person. A delegate is a person authorized and sent to represent others as in a meeting or team.

Delegation Days: Delegation Days are dates/days identified by leadership for the passing on or assigning of a task to others.

Delegation Day Schedule: A Delegation Day Schedule identifies specific days throughout the year for the delegation of tasks from one employee to another. A pre-determined and communicated Delegation Day Schedule enables manager oversight and planning of what can be delegated, from whom, and to whom, to ensure continuity of performance while providing cross-training opportunities for employees. A pre-determined and communicated Delegation Day Schedule also enables tracking of what is delegated/learned by each employee to ensure value and continued learning opportunities for each employee.

Dynamic Delegation: Dynamic Delegation™ is a program that enables the systematic delegation of tasks by each employee, enabling employees the choice to free themselves from old, tiresome tasks and gain free time to receive new tasks and learn new skills.

Dynamic Delegation Training for Managers: Training for managers in how to: 1) Think about and oversee Dynamic Delegation in their department; and 2) Interface with the Vitality Team for delegation tracking and employee opportunity development.

Dynamic Teaming: Dynamic Teaming is the ability to spontaneously combine employees from different departments, levels, and locations, who are trained in Vitality basics, and to collaborate on issue resolution and problem solving, new initiative planning, and real-time mentoring anywhere, anytime, as required by the situation.

Dynamic Delegation and Opportunity Tracking System: A leadership tool for Human Resource professionals to support managers in effective, efficient Dynamic Delegation™ and opportunity development for their employees.

Employee Engagement Opportunities: Opportunities to expand employee perspectives about the organization and their own possibilities.

Essence: See Strategic Essence.

Dynamic Employee Resource Planning: A traditional function (employee resource planning) with a new directive to build employee agility and flexibility in an organization.

Experiential Learning: Learning from real-time experience (not in a classroom or a book,) e.g., real-time listening to expert dialogue about planning or problem solving; hands-on training and mentoring (giving or receiving); visiting and developing relationships in departments adjacent to the employee's job; visiting and learning about other locations and functions, etc.

FLOW: Freedom to Learn, Observe, and Work. A clear mandate for Vitality.

Framework of Integrated Incentives: A construct to represent, describe, and communicate employee performance incentives clearly in an organization.

HR File: Human Resources file for each employee. Some organizations may not have a Human Resources Department or may outsource Human Resource functions, yet "HR File" is commonly used to refer to the files and records an organization maintains for its employees.

These files usually retain employee hiring and salary information, performance appraisals, and salary or bonus awards. They can and often do retain descriptions of difficult situations and negative reports. This file is the Organization's property and is often considered a clandestine tool for management of employee opportunity.

Horizontal Communication and Leadership: Leadership communication in an organization has two primary networks, vertical and horizontal. Horizontal communication is how the leader of a department implements communication to employees within a department. It also refers to how multiple departments communicate with each other, on what level, and with a specific purpose.

Incentive: Something that incites or tends to incite to action or greater effort, as a reward offered for increased effectiveness and efficiency.

Individual Assessment: The Vitalize software tool used to assess the level of Stagnancy versus level of Vitalization of individual employees in an organization embarking on the Vitalize Your Workforce program.

Inside Game: The work that must be accomplished on the inside individuals and organizations to effect sustainable transformation to a Vitalize state of being. Desired results cannot be purchased as an "item" on the outside.

Integrated Incentives: Combining desired performance and desired behaviors to build a Vitalized organization.

Mission Statement: One of the four Core Leadership Statements required to focus an organization to achieve a set of desired goals. The Mission Statement is closely related to the overall Vision Statement of where the organization is going. The Mission Statement provides a succinct view on how the goals will be achieved.

Language of a Department or Function: The terminology specific to that function. For example: Accounting "talks" in debits, credits, investments, and taxes. Shipping "talks" in truckload and LTL shipping, pallets, carriers, customs, and road fees.

Layered Incentives: Layered Incentives recognize very real differences exist in employee desires to further their careers, how they learn, how fast they learn, their levels of tolerance for change, their abilities to communicate, their fears, and their visions for their futures. These differences can be respectfully attributed to different cultures, different life experiences, or to differences in their very nature. Layered incentives start at easy, basic levels, and offer greater and greater opportunities to learn and participate depending on the employee's preference at the time. They can choose to stop where they are comfortable at the time, and reach again when they are more confident. The level and speed is up to them, without judgment. The employee management value here is that the progression is their choice.

Life-/Work-Value Application: Incentives that can benefit the employee at work, home, and in the community.

Living Fabric of Incentives: Incentives that are planned with flexible application to grow with each employee: his or her talents, interests, desires.

Meaningful Action: Hands-on learning, work opportunities, and rewards that have meaning to the employee.

Measurement: "You can't manage what you can't measure" is a fundamental management principle. The Vitalize Your Workforce approach places strong emphasis on measuring Stagnancy vs Vitalization as well as measuring overall strategic parameters. This emphasis allows for application of "the engineering approach" to Vitalization—a rigorous, reliable, reproducible method that delivers results.

Measuring Tools: The software tools used as part of the Vitalize Your Workforce approach to measure Stagnancy and Vitalization of individuals and organizational elements (business units).

Mentoring: A relationship in which a more experienced or more knowledgeable person helps to guide a less experienced or less knowledgeable person. The mentor may be older or younger than the person being mentored, but he or she must have a certain area of expertise.

Motivational Leadership: Leadership that connects with and engages employees in a way that encourages the employee to want to act or perform better.

Meaningful Reward: Reward is showing appreciation, providing a specific gift, or offering a new opportunity to an employee in return for work well done. Meaningful reward is respecting the way the employee would like to be recognized (fanfare/no fanfare) and providing a reward that is most beneficial to that particular employee at his or her particular time of life.

Meaningful Training: Training that provides real benefit to an employee's work and confidence and his ability to support his family and contribute more to his community.

Natural People-Leaders: People who have the innate ability to relate to and influence others to action. They:
- help others feel comfortable
- communicate openly and easily
- are natural role models:
- radiate a positive attitude
- demonstrate a non-judgmental, can-do attitude
- actively participating
- honor their innate sense of right and wrong
- effortlessly motivate others
- feel comfortable in their own skin
- stay open to new ideas
- often being versatile and resourceful
- thrive on teamwork

Natural people-leaders play vital roles with every organization. They often lack the formal education to be visible or use their innate leadership gifts to their full capacity. They have natural leadership talents versus "trained" or "assigned" leadership.

Open-Minded Inquiry: Inquiry with a true interest in the employee with no attachment to the answer, whether you think it is right or wrong, open or closed, big or small. Open-minded inquiry encourages the employee to ask questions, learn, and explore alternative answers/solutions without fear of judgment or detriment.

Organization Element (Business Unit): The component of an organization being modeled or managed during the Vitalize Your Workforce process.

Organization Element Assessment: The Vitalize Your Workforce software tool used to assess the level of Stagnancy versus Vitalization of any organization element (business unit).

Performance Levels: Levels of performance and behavior created to provide "reach," e.g., ways for the employee to experience more of whom he or she is while contributing more and more to the organization's benefit.

Permission: Authorization granted to do something; formal consent.

Perspective: From the Latin root meaning "look through" or "perceive," a particular way of considering something. Perspectives are based on experience, i.e., what one has seen, heard, felt, actions taken, etc.

Perspective Expansion: The providing of new knowledge or experience that changes the way a person perceives his or her life, relationships, opportunities, etc.

Policy Statement: The fourth of four Core Leadership Statements required to focus an organization to achieve a set of desired goals. Clearly defined Policies guide an organization's actions and behaviors to manage the leadership-employee relationship, peer-to-peer relationship, and organization to supplier/customer and investor relationships. Policies provide the guidelines and expectations for participation and the boundaries required to ensure the actions and behaviors meet the quality, respect, and responsibility requirements.

Potential: The latent human qualities or abilities of an employee that may be developed and lead to future success or usefulness.

Progressive Thinking, Learning Organization: An organization with an internally produced charter to evolve thinking, learning, managing, and implementing new ways to be more successful with the products, services, people development, image, and influence that form the business' essence.

Quantum-Leap Thinking: Willingness to identify what is standard or common thinking that keeps an organization producing standard results, and reaching beyond that thinking to new ideas, actions, and perspectives that produce greater, more progressive results.

Reductionist Thinking: Part of the ideas set forth by Frederick Winslow Taylor in his book *The Principles of Scientific Management* (1997) that express production efficiencies are gained through standardization on the production level guided by statistical analysis and direction provided from the top. This idea soon translated to the best are at the top coupled with thinking about the rest of the staff complement as "just workers." Today, we know this is not true, nor can it remain as a guiding principle if companies want to evolve to highly resilient, competitive, Vitalized organizations. Reductionist thinking has played a significant role in crushing human initiative in many organizations, thereby contributing significantly to stagnation.

Reach: The stretching out as an arm in a specified direction in order to touch or grasp something. The expansion of effort toward something desired or beneficial.

Reward Visibility: The offering of rewards in a manner that makes them visible, able to be acknowledged by others, and received in a way that makes them an education for others, e.g., presenting what the employee accomplished to receive the reward.

Rungs on a Ladder: An analogy relating to how employees feel: stuck in a fixed sequence of positions, with many positions ahead, and in a position where delegation is only handed downward.

Stagnation-Vitalization Rating: The rating of Stagnation versus Vitalization generated by application of the Vitalize Your Workforce software tools.

Strategy: The essence of the organization and how it thrives—this is the fundamental meaning of the term "strategy" that is widely used and frequently misunderstood.

Strategic Essence: The fundamental raison d'etre of an organization—the fundamental driver that underpins the organization's formation, growth, and success. The element that the organization's founders most fundamentally had in focus. The core differentiator in terms of which the organization thrives, prospers, and succeeds in its vision and mission.

Shining Star (inside): The core energy and intelligence inherent in each human being.

"Soft Start" (for an employee learning a new skill): A gentle, short step from where a person's talents are now to learning and doing something more or different.

Stagnating Employee: An employee who is demotivated, alienated, disloyal, not creatively engaged with his job, wishes he were somewhere else, and only remains because he cannot find a better alternative. A stagnant employee is a "lost" employee.

Standard Performance Level: Relates to the first or baseline level of performance in the Vitalize Your Workforce Integrated Incentives Program. This is the starting point for acceptable performance.

Standard Performance Level Rewards: The employee rewards available/planned for employees accomplishing the Standard Performance Level.

StratSnap© (Strategic Snapshot) is a Vitalize Your Workforce process developed by Dr. James Robertson that utilizes a proprietary software tool to record, compare, analyze, prioritize, and help align participant views (positive and negative) on any subject.

Talent Development Initiatives: Programs designed to increase employee interest, participation, and productivity.

Thrive: An organization thrives by doing the right things well. The Vitalize Your Workforce approach focuses on assisting the organization to thrive by focusing on the core people issues of Stagnation and Vitalization that underpin the organization's viability and success.

Value Beyond Measure: The inherent value of a reward, recognition, gift, surprise, or occurrence. Confidence, joy, willing collaboration, and enthusiasm are examples of value beyond measure.

Vertical Leadership: Leadership communication in an organization has two primary networks, vertical and horizontal. Vertical communication is top-down communication, with feedback traveling back up often through the same specifically designated points of contact.

Vision Statement: A published description and declaration of what an organization does, what it stands for, where it is going, and where it wants to be in the future.

Vitality:

  a. Individual Vitality: Enthusiastic personal interest and energy for greater participation in learning new aspects about one's job, organization, skills, greater collaboration, and contribution.

  b. Organization Vitality: The degree of aliveness and participation of employees and management to collaborate easily, quickly, and enthusiastically to achieve more significant results.

Vitality Circles: Formal activity sessions in each function that provide a local forum for employees to practice and apply the Core Skills they are learning with encouragement, mentoring, and recognition.

Vitality of Possibility ™: The springing up of energy, interest, vitality, and verve resulting from openings to do more, create more, become more. The intrigue of being able to do more, learn more, experience more of our dreams, experience more of our natural talents, and become more of whom we really are!

Vitalizing Your Workforce: Creating a leadership of culture, enthusiasm, and participation for what the business or organization, and all those working in it, can become. Exponentially multiplying resiliency, interest, creativity, collaboration, and new exhilarating results, from the inside out.

Vitalization Index: Numeric index computed by the Vitalize Your Workforce Assessment Tools as an indication of the level of Vitalization of an employee or organizational entity. Scale of 0 to 10 where 0 = totally stagnant (could not be worse) and 10 = totally vitalized (could not be better).

Vitalize Leadership Team: A leadership team designated to apply the principles of Vitalize Your Workforce throughout the organization to eliminate stagnation and stimulate employee vitality, including learning, participation, confidence, and commitment to expand employees' contribution and potential. It is distinct from the Human Resources function.

Urgency: Importance, insistence, necessity, need, pressure, stress, hurry, rush.

Willing Collaboration: Confidence in being able to contribute to a team or an endeavor; openness to join a conversation, project, problem-solving team, and positive outlook on being able to contribute something worthwhile as an individual and collectively as a team. Willing collaboration = positive, enthusiastic teamwork.

RESEARCH REFERENCES

1 Huggins, Kathleen. "Is Your Organization Change Agile?," Mercer Peoplepro Blog, March 27, 2017. https://blog.mercerpeoplepro.com/organization-change-agile/

2 Waitzkin, Joshua. "Conversations on Creativity with Repeat Bloomer Joshua Waitzkin," Interview by Scott Barry Kaufman PhD, Beautiful Minds, Nov 27, 2008. https://www.psychologytoday.com/blog/beautiful-minds/200811/conversations-creativity-repeat-bloomer-joshua-waitzkin

3 "State of The American Work Place," Gallup, 2013, http://www.michaeljbeck.com/documents/State percent20of percent20the percent20American percent20Workplace percent20Report percent202013.pdf

4 "State of the American Workplace study," Gallup quoted in "A disturbing 70 percent of employees are not engaged in their jobs," Maxwell & Locke Ritter, http://www.mlrpc.com/articles/a-disturbing-70-percent-of-employees-are-not-engaged-in-their-jobs/

5 De Silva, Zac. "BEST WORKPLACES – Increase your profits by up to 2.5 times!" Business Changing, July 3, 2011, http://www.businesschanging.com/businesscoaching-increase-your-profits-by-up-to-2-5-times/

6 De Silva, Zac. "BEST WORKPLACES—Increase your profits by up to 2.5 times!" Business Changing, July 3, 2011, http://www.businesschanging.com/businesscoaching-increase-your-profits-by-up-to-2-5-times/

7 "How Full Is Your Bucket? Research," Gallup, http://strengths.gallup.com/114088/full-bucket-research.aspx

8 "Coaching Employees for High Performance," Quantum Workplace file https://community.cengage.com/GECResource2/cfs-file/__key/telligent-evolution-components-attachments/01-13-00-00-00-01-57-24/Coaching_2D00_Employees_2D00_for_2D00_High_2D00_Performance.pdf

9 "2016 Human Capital Benchmarking Report," SHRM, 2016, 16, https://www.shrm.org/hr-today/trends-and-forecasting/research-and-surveys/Documents/2016-Human-Capital-Report.pdf

10 Covert, Bryce. "The Economic Devastation Fueling The Anger In Baltimore," ThinkProgress, April 28, 2015. https://thinkprogress.org/the-economic-devastation-fueling-the-anger-in-baltimore-8511b97c0630/

11 Dr. James Robertson, "Strategic Snapshot Tool," Dr. James Robertson, http://www.james-a-robertson-and-associates.com/Strategy/StratSnapTool.aspx

12 bid.

13 Ibid.

14 Ibid.

15 Murphy, Margot. Case Study on Consulting Assignment, 2012.

16 Murphy, Margot. Case Study in a Communications Company, 2000.

17 Bureau of Labor Statistics quoted in Gary Topchik, "Managing workplace negativity," 2000.

18 Pearson, Christine. "The Price of Incivility," Harvard Business Review, Jan 2013. https://hbr.org/2013/01/the-price-of-incivility

19 Bowersox, Kathy "Why Employee Engagement Matters," Allen Austin, May 1, 2017. https://allenaustin.com/employee-engagement-matters/

20 ASAE, Center for Association Leadership, www.asaecenter.org

21 Newell-Legner, Ruby. "Understanding Customers," https://www.helpscout.net/75-customer-service-facts-quotes-statistics/

22 Toby Graham CFPB, Complaints, "How Complaints Can Make Your Business More Competitive," Compli, June 21, 2017. https://www.compli.com/blog/cfpb-requirements-can-be-competitive-advantages/

23 Lee Resources quoted in Stephane Bourque, "Just how important are customer experiences?" Incognito, April 14, 2015. http://www.incognito.com/blog/just-how-important-are-customer-experiences/

24 Customer Experience Impact Report by Harris Interactive/ Right Now, 2010 quoted in Phyllis Gillman, "4 Ways to Improve Your Problem Solving Skills," Vertafore, October 12, 2016. http://www.vertafore.com/Resources/Blog/4-Ways-to-Improve-Your-Problem-Solving-Skills

25 Google Dictionary

26 Gallo, Amy. "Why Aren't You Delegating?" Harvard Business Review, July 26, 2012, https://hbr.org/2012/07/why-arent-you-delegating

27 Webster's Dictionary

28 Ibid.

29 Vorhauser-Smith, Sylvia. "How the Best Places to Work Are Nailing Employee Engagement," Forbes, Aug. 14, 2013. https://www.forbes.com/sites/sylviavorhausersmith/2013/08/14/how-the-best-places-to-work-are-nailing-employee-engagement/#57f870ff5cc7

30 Public/Private Ventures study of Big Brothers Big Sisters quoted in "Why mentoring: mentoring impact," Mentor, http://www.mentoring.org/why-mentoring/mentoring-impact/

31 "Why mentoring: mentoring impact," Mentor, http://www.mentoring.org/why-mentoring/mentoring-impact/

32 de Janasz, Suzanne. Maury Peiperl, "CEOs Need Mentors Too," Harvard Business Review, April 2015, https://hbr.org/2015/04/ceos-need-mentors-too

33 Span, Scott. "Something You Should Know: 65 percent of Your Workforce Is Looking For a New Job," Tolero Solutions, September 15, 2015. https://www.tlnt.com/something-you-should-know-65-of-your-workforce-is-looking-for-a-new-job/

34 Maslow, Dr. Abraham. "Maslow's hierarchy of needs" quoted in Michelle Morrison-Valfre, "Foundations of Mental Health Care," 2013, 46.

35 Bead, Richard. Vice-president of human resources for TELUS Corp quoted in Almas Sabir, "Reward and Recognition System-Key Behaviors to Benefit Employees and Businesses in Competitive Job Markets," American Research Journal of Business and Management, no.2 (2016), 2. https://www.arjonline.org/papers/arjbm/v2-i1/12.pdf

36 Adkins, Amy and Brandon Rigoni, "Managers: Millennials Want Feedback, but Won't Ask for It," Gallup, June 2, 2016. http://news.gallup.com/businessjournal/192038/managers-millennials-feedback-won-ask.aspx

37 Ann Hewlett, Sylvia. "Use the Right Incentives for Gen Y, Gen X, and Boomers," HBR ideacast, 14 Dec. 2011. https://www.conference-board.org/blog/post.cfm?post=167

38 CampusAuction, "Altruism Drives Millennials—Doing Good Can Help the World—and the Bottom Line, Says CampusAuction," Nov 28 2012, http://www.prweb.com/releases/2012/11/prweb10176566.htm

39 "Freedom to Learn, Observe, and Work"

40 Undercover Boss, a CBS television production

41 Beyond Resilience, LLC, 2016

42 Murphy, Robertson, and Vogel StratSnap© Analysis, 2017

43 Ibid.

44 Beyond Resilience, LLC, 2017

45 James A. Robertson and Associates, 2014

46 Professor Malcolm McDonald, Professor Malcolm McDonald MA (Oxon) MSc PhD DLitt DSc Emeritus Professor, Cranfield University School of Management. Personal communication with James Robertson, 1992

47 James Robertson and Associates, 2003

48 Daimler Chrysler, "Daimler Chrysler post merger integration", https://lawaspect.com/daimler-chrysler/

49 James A. Robertson and Associates, 2005

50 Sinek, Simon. http://startwithwhy.com

51 "Publix Super Market, Inc.: A Customer Service Leader", 2012, http://www.icmrindia.org/casestudies/catalogue/Marketing/MKTG296.htm

52 Gallup, Tom Rath and Donald Clifton, "How Full Is Your Bucket? Positive Strategies for Work and Life," 2001

53 "Campbell Soup Company Case Study," Heman Miller, https://www.hermanmiller.com/content/dam/hermanmiller/documents/case_studies/CS_CAM_FULL.pdf

54 Towers Perrin quoted in Kevin Kruse, "What Is Employee Engagement," Forbes, JUN 22, 2012, https://www.forbes.com/sites/kevinkruse/2012/06/22/employee-engagement-what-and-why/#607fd0947f37

55 Kenexa, 2009 study quoted in Joel Oleson, "The Rise of the Enterprise Social Consultant," Wired, Nov 2013, https://www.wired.com/insights/2013/11/the-rise-of-the-enterprise-social-consultant/

56 Kevin Kruse, "What Is Employee Engagement," Forbes, Jun 22, 2012, https://www.forbes.com/sites/kevinkruse/2012/06/22/employee-engagement-what-and-why/#607fd0947f37

57 Vogel, Dan. Beyond Resilience, LLC: case study with a manufacturing company

58 James A. Robertson, James A. Robertson and Associates

59 Robertson, James A. 2016

60 Ibid.

INDEX

A

Ability to Lead People, 247

Adams, John Quincy, xviii Addressing negativity, 62, 64

Adelaja, Sunday, 78

Agile, 19, 72, 266, 293, 305

Appreciation, 113–121, 127, 144, 175–177, 187, 224, 293, 299

Appreciation Files: Appreciation File Program, 117–120, 293; Employee Appreciation Files, 293

Appreciative Inquiry, 294

Assessment, 31–32, 187, 255, 257–258, 263, 273, 275, 282, 294, 298, 300, 304

Association for Talent Development (ATD), 293

AT&T Pioneer Program, 94

B

Basic Standard Performance, 164

Benefits of Mentoring, 100

Benefits of Personalization, 118

Bi-Pole Measures, 254

Biro, Meghan, 100, 102

Broad, Eli, 86

Business Unit, 30, 196, 255, 257, 294, 299–300

C

C-LEVELS, 28

Campbell's Soup, 218, 223–225

Capacity to do better, 294

Carnegie, Dale, 122

Cascading communication, 294

Cascading Your Key Leadership Statements, 294

Cloud, Glenda, 180

Collaborative sense of purpose, 209, 211, 295

Conant, Doug, 218, 225

Considerations for Future Perfect: Empowered People, 268–269; Increased Shareholder Value, 271–272; Integrated Team Leadership Philosophy, 272–273; Strategic Measurements, 270; Vitality Circles, 273–274; Vitality Leadership, 269–270; Vitality Metrics, 271

Continual Opportunity, 95, 133–137, 157, 168, 269

Contributing Mission Statement, 211, 295

Core Emotions, 144

Corporate Vitality Team Oversight, 136, 156

Covey, Stephen R., 172

Crabtree, Steve, 279

Credit Card Model, 161–162, 295

Critical Factors for Success: Effective Business Integration, 284; Effective

Engineering Solution Design, 284;
Effective Executive Custody, 284 ;
Effective Measurement and Data, 284;
Effective Strategic Definition, 284;
Reliable Technology, 285

Critical Issue Resolution, 69, 71, 73, 75, 77

Cross-training, 81–82, 92, 163–164, 187–188, 270, 273, 295–296

Cultural Guidelines, 219; and leadership team values, 228–229

Culture statement, 228, 230, 296

D

Dangerous Predicament, 102

de Montesquieu, Charles, 262

de Silva, Zac, 3

Dead-end Managers, 296

DeJesus, Noel, 132

Delegation, 88–93

Delegation Day Schedule, 93, 296

Delegation Days, 93, 296

Discordant Communication, 28

Drucker, Peter, 26–27, 253

Dynamic Delegation, 87–95, 165, 187, 245, 296–297

Dynamic Delegation Training, 91–92, 297

Dynamic Teaming, 94, 297

E

Effective Appreciation, 117

Einstein, Albert, 34

Employee disengagement, 255, 278–279

Employee Engagement, 1, 11, 102, 218, 224–225, 297, 306, 308, 315

Employee Engagement Opportunities, 297

Employee Stagnation, 1–5, 9–13, 15, 21–22, 63, 87–88, 95, 120, 133, 144, 189, 221, 229, 255, 270, 280, 282, 290, 293, 296, 315

Energetic Mentoring, 245, 290

Engineering against Failure, 281

engineering Factors for Success, 280

Enterprise Resource Planning (ERP), 13, 197

Expanded opportunity, 83, 175

Expanding individual potential, 105

Expansion of Perspective, 87, 99

F

Factors Causing Business Improvement Failure: Failure to Address Soft Issues, 282; Ineffective Executive Custody, 282; Lack of Accurate, 282; Lack of an Engineering Approach, 283; Lack of Effective Strategic Alignment, 282; Mythology, 281; Technology Issues, 283

Ferriss, Timothy, 140

Focus on Vitality, 13, 22, 220, 229

Franklin, Benjamin, 46, 80, 315

Freedom to Learn, Observe and Work (FLOW), 20–21, 23, 40, 57, 88–89, 93, 95, 153, 193, 222, 243, 297

Freire, Paul, 242

Future Perfect, 263, 268, 275

G

Gap, 154, 195, 244, 256, 258, 264, 275

Gens X, Y, and Z, 101

Goldratt, Eli, 252, 254

Gore, Al, 234

H

High Pass-Along Goodwill, 94

High-level Opportunity Rewards, 165

Horizontal Communication and Leadership, 298
Human Resources (HR) Files, 115, 120, 293

I

Iacocca, Lee, 110
IBM Consulting Group, 28
Incentive Challenge, 143
Incentive Plan, 161
Individual Employee Vitalization, 257
Integrated Incentives, 4, 136, 141, 153, 157, 163–169, 173, 187, 269, 297–298, 303
Integrated Incentives Honors, 153
Integrated Incentives program, 162, 303
Intrinsic Motivation, 142

K

Kotter, John P., 92, 95

L

Lack of Employee Engagement, 102, 224, 315
Language of a department, 298
Lawrence, 225–228
Layered Incentives, 143, 298–299
Leadership behaviors, 166
Leadership Goals, 106
Leadership Team values, 228
Leading for Vitality, 23, 289
learn & practice Core Skills, 164
Line-Timing System, 41
Living Fabric of Incentives, 153, 155, 157, 168, 299

M

Maryland Teachers Union, 123
Maslow's Hierarchy of Needs, 124–125, 307
Maslow, Abraham, 124
Maxwell, John, 288
McChrystal, Stanley, 87, 214, 245, 272
McDonald, Malcolm, xiv, 193, 307
McMackin, Ron, 226–227
McNamara, Robert, 112
Meaningful Action, 145–146, 299
Meaningful Rewards, 173–175, 177, 188, 299
Meaningful Training, 154–155, 157, 300
Measuring Tools, 4, 28, 299
Medium Level participation, 165
Mission statement, 209–215, 222, 271, 295, 298
Motivational Leadership, 143, 244, 299
Mridha, Debasish, 10, 18
Mulcahy, Anne M., 152
Multi-skilling, 81
Mutual Permission, 134

N

Naam, Ramez, 138
Natural People-Leaders, 41–42, 50, 52, 73, 92, 166, 168, 230, 238–239, 243–247, 289, 300
New Paradigm Program, 66
New Sustainable Approach, 74

O

Open-Door Policies, 70, 72
Open-minded inquiry, 223, 300
Opportunity Tracking System, 297

Organization Element, 30–31, 294, 300
Organization Element Assessment, 31, 300
Organizational Entity Vitalization, 257
Organizational Improvement Industry, 286

P

Performance appraisals, 114–115, 120, 298
Performance Levels, 301
Permission, 19, 23, 40–43, 50, 74–75, 93–94, 133–134, 155, 164, 166, 175, 223, 301
Pertinent Questions, 72
Plank, Kevin, 250
Policy Statement, 118, 156, 301
Porter, Michael, 193
Powell, Colin, 36
Problem-Solving Language, 51
Problem-Solving Practice, 49
Problem-Solving Process, 40, 42–43, 51–52, 64, 73
Problem-Solving Skill Training, 73
Progressive Incentives, 139, 141, 164, 188
Progressive thinking, 5, 23, 43, 58, 73, 75, 87, 95, 104, 106, 119, 124, 129–130, 136, 143, 162–163, 167, 169, 174–176, 183, 202–206, 212–215, 221, 225, 230–231, 237–238, 269, 301

Q

Quantum-Leap Thinking, 87, 95, 301

R

Real People-Leaders, 243, 245, 247
Reductionism, 13
Reductionist thinking, 13–14, 301–302

Reward Visibility, 302
Robertson, James, 6, 182, 192, 303, 305, 307
Robertson, James A., 20, 23, 307–308
Rungs on a ladder, 88, 302

S

Second Attention Span, 116, 293
Sequential Performance, 163
Seven Critical Concerns, 29
Shared Learning, 4, 79, 81–85, 88, 105, 163–164, 168, 187–188, 229, 245, 269, 273, 289
Sinek, Simon, 160, 210
Soft Issues, 27–28, 256, 258, 280, 282
Soft start, 302
Stagnant Organization, 264–268
Stagnating employee, 302
Stagnation Crisis, 22
Stagnation-Vitalization Rating, 30, 302
Standard Performance Level, 164, 168, 302–303
Standard Performance Level Rewards, 303
Strategic Essence: Benefits of Strategic Essence, 196 ; Discovering Strategic Essence, 195 ; Ignoring Strategic Essence, 194, 196 ; Lack of Strategic Essence, 194; Role of Strategic Essence in Vitalizing, 197; What IS Strategic Essence, 193; Why is it Vital?, 194
Strategy, xiii, 4, 192–194, 210, 223, 244, 290, 302, 305, 307
StratSnap, 28, 32, 43, 303, 307
Suggestion Boxes, 70–72
Supply chains, 55, 58

T

Talent Development Initiatives, 303
Taylor, Frederick Winslow, 13, 301
Team of Teams, 87, 214, 272
Technology Innovation, 194
The inside game, 104
The Principles of Scientific Management, 13, 301
Thrive, 73, 192–193, 195–196, 202, 229, 236, 265, 271, 300, 302–303
Thriving Organization, 264–268
Timely issue resolution, 219
True Problem Solver, 38

U

Udall, Stewart, 8
Underlying Problem, 115
Urgency, 214, 304

V

Value Beyond Measure, 303
Vertical Leadership, 303
Vision statement, 201–206, 209, 298, 303
Vitality Circles, 273-274
Vitality Guarantees Success, 289, 291
Vitality of Possibility, 91, 146, 163, 304
Vitality opportunities, 162
Vitalization Index, 188, 304
Vitalize Issue Resolution Process, 39, 162
Vitalize Leadership Team, 304
Vitalize Organizational Entity Assessment, 258
Vitalize Your Focus, 251

Vitalize Your Workforce (VYW) program techniques: Critical Concerns Process, 30; Critical Objectives, 30; Stagnation-Vitalization rating for the Organization, 30; Stagnation-Vitalization rating of individual employees, 30–31; Stagnation-Vitalization rating of Organization Elements, 30
Vitalized employees, 19, 21, 23, 167, 224, 274
Vitalizing Your Policies, 238
Vitalizing Your Workforce, 4, 42–43, 83, 107, 120, 128, 155, 197–198, 238, 246–247, 253, 258, 279–287, 304

W

Waitzkin, Joshua, 1, 305
Welch, Jack, 208
Well-planned incentives, 144
Willing Collaboration, 221, 303–304
Winch, Guy, 62
Winfrey, Oprah, 98
Work-Life Balance, 294
workforce Stagnation-Vitalization, 31

ABOUT THE AUTHOR

MARGOT MURPHY IS A PENNSYLVANIA NATIVE AND A FORMER sports competitor with twenty-seven years extensive experience in management and leadership with global Fortune 100 Corporations. Margot has a passion for excellence, teamwork, and creating and building things that work. Her passion was set early in life with a quote from Benjamin Franklin: "If there is one way of doing things, there is always a better way." She practices this philosophy wherever she goes, creating paths of proven success in eleven start-ups, four turn-arounds, and in ongoing businesses. She has a natural talent for netting complex situations down to the core turning points, setting clear visions and missions, and simplifying the priorities to reach a goal.

Margot's passion is encouraging people to expand and experience their full potential, whether on a sports team, or as part of a business organization. After her formal retirement from direct corporate life, she became more aware of the pervasive business issue of "lack of employee engagement." The repeating statistics that 85 percent of employees are disengaged, with high turnover and negativity in an accelerating market that needs committed employees more than ever, were painful.

To learn the roots of the issue first hand, Margot spent a year traveling around the country giving a variety of seminars in fifteen different states, to over 2,400 participants. The underlying cause of lack of engagement became clear—the root is personal employee stagnation. Lack of engagement is only a symptom. Realizing this truth, Margot knew it was time to lend her voice and her experience to find a better way—for both business leaders and their employees.

Margot chose the word "vitality" as the core of her work because it means "life force," "the capacity to live and develop." Vitality is more than the now common terms of flexibility and agility. Margot believes Vitality is the essence of new goals for leadership, for those businesses that see the current problem and are looking for a solution—a new competitive edge. In *Vitalize Your Workforce*, Margot has once again simplified a complex problem into core turning points, and has set a clear Vision and Mission for business leaders, with supporting programs for Vitality.

HIRE THE
Vitalize Your Workforce
EXPERTS

Vitality Leadership Consulting | Vitality Measuring | Strategic Planning
Corporate Strategic Learning | Vitality Leadership Certification (in process)

The world is moving fast. Markets and technologies are accelerating. You need a workforce that is alert, willing, present, and ready to meet your needs.

Are you losing time and money because your employees are looking the other way?
Are your employees busy—but disconnected?

IF YOU WANT TO LEARN THE TRUTH ABOUT EMPLOYEE STAGNATION, CALL US!

- We help you understand the true cause(s) of employee lack of engagement.
- We provide more than just a program. We provide a framework for instilling Vitality leadership and reducing the long-term drag of employee stagnation.
- We help you build a new sustainable competitive edge with employee potential already there—but asleep.

Are you a startup?

Learn and embed the basics so you can be ahead of the game from the start.

Are you a long-established company?

Let us help introduce Vitality Leadership principles and practices that respect your current structure and help you leverage it more effectively for a new day.

Are you planning to redesign your company for greater future strength?

Call us to ensure you don't carry the same underlying employee stagnation problems forward with you into your new design.

ASK US ABOUT:

- Executive Consulting and Coaching
- Corporate Vitality Assessments
- Strategic Planning/Operations Planning
- Vitality ERP
- Advanced Data Analytics
- Corporate Strategic Learning
- HR transition from purely administration to Vitality partners
- Change Management and ROI

To schedule an appointment and share your interests, email: CEO@vitalizeyourworkforce.com

www.ingramcontent.com/pod-product-compliance
Lightning Source LLC
Chambersburg PA
CBHW052053110526
44591CB00013B/2185